Printing and
for Sc

Samuel Jesse Vaughn

Alpha Editions

This edition published in 2024

ISBN 9789362514592

Design and Setting By
Alpha Editions
www.alphaedis.com
Email - info@alphaedis.com

Contents

INTRODUCTION - 1 -

THE ART OF PRINTING - 3 -

TYPE SETTING - 11 -

RULES OF COMPOSITION - 22 -

PROOF MARKS - 23 -

IMPOSITION - 24 -

PRESSWORK - 33 -

CLEANING AND DISTRIBUTING - 36 -

WHAT TO PRINT AND HOW TO PROCEED - 39 -

METHOD OF TEACHING THE LOWER CASE - 42 -

WOOD CUTS AND METAL PLATES - 43 -

THE EQUIPMENT—ITS SELECTION AND COST - 47 -

ARRANGEMENT AND DISPOSITION OF EQUIPMENT - 62 -

INTRODUCTION - 71 -

CLASSES OF BINDINGS. - 73 -

II. CASE BINDING. - 74 -

III. LIBRARY BINDING. - 84 -

IV. EXTRA BINDING. - 93 -

V. REBINDING. - 104 -

VI. EQUIPMENT. - 108 -

VII. SUGGESTIVE COURSE. - 111 -

FIRST GRADE. - 115 -

SECOND GRADE. - 116 -

THIRD GRADE. - 117 -

FOURTH GRADE.   - 122 -

FIFTH GRADE.   - 125 -

SIXTH GRADE.   - 128 -

SEVENTH GRADE.   - 132 -

EIGHTH GRADE.   - 134 -

INTRODUCTION

Printing as a Manual Art in Schools.

Woodwork has been quite generally introduced into the high school and grammar school. With all the defects of the earlier presentation of the subject, not to speak of those in later efforts, it has made a surprisingly general appeal, and has met with unusual and deserved success. Some of the methods employed, tending to place a ban on originality and thought, have brought it far short of its possibilities in the aid of intellectual development. To a considerable extent the woodwork has not touched, as intimately as it might, the vital interests of the pupils and of the homes; and, by its own limitations, it has not had an especially strong social bearing. The need is not less woodwork but more original and thoughtful woodwork, and also a greater variety of other constructive work which touches more and wider interests and which may appeal to those not particularly adapted to that one line. In this way it will be possible to strengthen the places where woodwork is weak. So far experience with printing in school indicates that it makes quite as general and permanent an appeal as woodwork.

Printing makes this very strong appeal to the boys because, in the first place, the printshop comes as near to reproducing a great world industry in the school as any other line of industrial work. Instead of doing simply the "roustabout" work of the beginning apprentice the boys are put to work with the regular shop equipment, and soon are ready to begin turning out some printing. It is a common thing to hear a boy remark, "This is just the way they do it down town." So they look upon printing as the work of real men, and feel that they are actually taking part in some of the activities that are potent in the affairs of men. It's wonderful, the pull of this feeling of participation in the world's work.

Besides this, there is probably no other line of Manual Arts work in which pupils, grade boys especially, get so practical a working knowledge of the actual shop work as in printing. This fact is often turned to good advantage by the boys, for there can scarcely be found a commercial printshop anywhere which is not glad to employ one or two boys during vacation time, if they know a little about the work and are interested.

There is the still further fact that printing offers the concrete embodiment of rules of punctuation, capitalization, syllabication, sentence structure, paragraphing, etc. It is an indisputable fact that work in the printshop influences in a remarkable way the disposition to observe good form and to follow the best usage in all such matters. It is a daily occurrence in the school printshop that some boy brings a text book or newspaper to exhibit what he considers a glaring disregard of some of these principles of composition.

Printing furnishes a distinctly different type of motor activity from woodwork, for it is the arrangement of certain unyielding forms within limited space to produce some desired effect.

In the matter of social significance printing is practically ideal. Almost every problem is a community project, that is, a number of pupils combine their efforts to produce it. Practically every task in the printshop is undertaken with the consciousness of real service to a great number of people in the school or in the community at large.

It is interesting to note that among the boys in school, the genuine joy in the production of printed matter does not necessarily arise out of a sense of the commercial value of the product. The class that has printed and illustrated a little pamphlet of stories for the second or third grade are proud and happy immeasurably beyond the pride and happiness that would come from a job of office blanks worth so many dollars. In other words, they are happy to the extent that the quality of their work merits praise, and that they feel able to make others happy by their services.

The school paper is an enterprise of very much the same nature. It is a real influence and a genuine service performed for which they expect no individual return except in the appreciation of those they serve, and pride in the excellence of their work and the skill it shows. This is certainly a kind of training for which there is a distinct need just now.

There is no other one of the Manual Arts that can touch so intimately the varied classwork, interests, and activities of school life as does printing, especially when combined with bookbinding.

It brings a freshness and vigor to the elementary reading and language work; it touches the athletics and social activities through announcements, programs, and notices in the school paper; it becomes an important factor in the celebration of special days, and in the preparation of material bearing on them; and it bears an intimate and vital relation to art.

Another interesting development is in the relation of printing to the other lines of constructive work. It has proved extremely valuable to have the completed problems written up in descriptive articles by the pupils, and to have the best of these compositions printed.

THE ART OF PRINTING

Methods and Tools of Composition.

In printing, composition includes all the steps from receiving the copy until the type is set up, proofed, corrected, and made up into page forms.

This discussion presupposes a knowledge of spelling, syllabication, punctuation, paragraphing, etc., all of which good composition really includes. Practical rules bearing on these different phases may be found in various handbooks for the printer.

The first essential in printing is, of course, a quantity of type properly arranged.

Type is cast from a composition of metals—lead, tin, antimony, and sometimes copper. This composition is melted and poured into moulds the size and shape of the desired type.

Accuracy in Size of Type. Lead is used as the chief constituent of the composition, because it shrinks very little in cooling. This makes greater accuracy possible. Accuracy is an absolute essential in type, for thousands of pieces of metal must be held together in one form by a slight pressure at the sides and ends of the form.

Lead alone is too soft to wear well and to retain the shape of the type under the constant pressure of the printing press. Tin is added to give hardness, and antimony or copper to give toughness to the type metal.

Type Described. Type are small columns of the metal with a letter or character in relief on one end of each column, as at Fig. 1. The surface of this relief portion from which the letter or character is printed is called the face.

The various faces are distinguished by names applied by the foundries, as "Caslon Old Style," "Engraver's Old English," "Banker's Script," etc.

The extreme length of type from the face to the foot is .918 inches, or about eleven-twelfths of an inch.

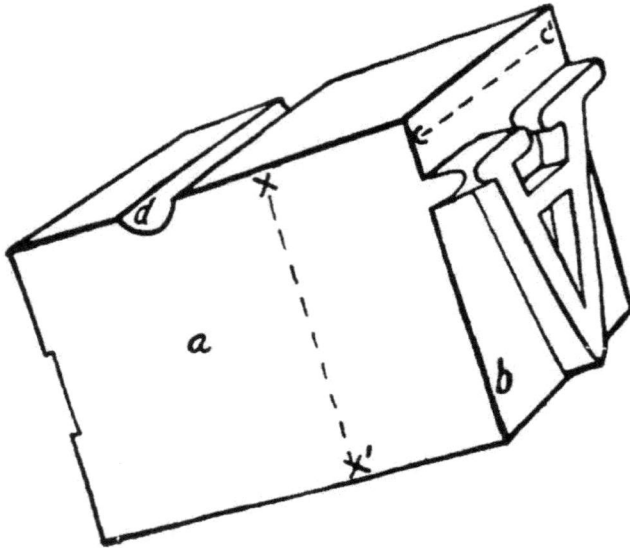

Fig. 1.

The column of metal on which the letter or character rests is the body or shank of the type (a, Fig. 1) and the distance which the body extends beyond the edge of the letter or character is the shoulder (b, Fig. 1).

On the side of the body next the base of the letter or character are one or more nicks (d, Fig. 1). The chief purpose of such nicks is to indicate the base of the letter or character, and thus to aid the compositor in keeping the type right side up without constantly referring to the face of the type.

To the manufacturer, these nicks indicate other things in addition to that mentioned above, but these need not be detailed here.

The size of the type has to do with the body, and signifies the vertical distance through the body, or the distance from the nick side to the opposite side, as from x to x′, Fig. 1.

Of course it is clear that among the large amount of type manufactured, there must be a great number of different faces on the same size of body; and that there may be two or three sizes of the same face on the same size of body.

In order to indicate a specific type, it is necessary to mention its size and the name by which that particular face is distinguished; as, "10 point Author's Roman Wide," "18 point Pabst Old Style," "6 point Caslon Bold Italic," etc.

The Point System. The type manufacturers of this country have adopted a uniform scale of sizes known as the point system. In this scheme, the unit or point is .0138 inches, or about one seventy-second part of an inch. The size of any type is so many points based upon this system. Twelve points constitute an *em pica* which is the larger unit of measurement.

When the printer speaks of dimensions, like the length and width of a page, he says it is a certain number of ems or picas long and wide. An em pica is one-sixth of an inch; so a page three inches by five inches is eighteen by thirty ems pica.

Until comparatively recent years there was no definite standard of type sizes. Each foundry established its own standards. If a printer wished to use type from different foundries, it probably was necessary to make some troublesome adjustments with bits of paper or otherwise to get them to line properly. (Specimen of words out of line.)

There was a sufficient similarity in sizes of type to justify the use of names to indicate certain sizes. The names used to designate the common sizes from 4½ to 12 point type according to the point system, are as follows:

4½   points—Diamond

5   points—Pearl

5½   points—Agate

6   points—Nonpareil

7   points—Minion

8   points—Brevier

9	points—Bourgeois
10	points—Long Primer
11	points—Small pica
12	points—Pica

1. This line is set in 6 point Caslon Bold.

2. This line is set in 8 point Post.

3. This line is set in 10 point Author's Roman Italic.

4. This line is set in 12 point Strathmore Old Style.

Some of these names, such as Nonpareil, Brevier, Long Primer, and Pica, are still in quite general use.

Not only is the height or depth of the body determined by the point system, but the width or set of the body (cc′ Fig. 1) is also cast on the point basis. There are no fractional points in the width of type made on the point set basis. Any number of letters or characters placed side by side make an integral number of points. This is called point set.

Also, in case a number of differently faced type with the same body are used in the same line, they are so cast that the different faces line with each other as well as if they were all of the same face.

The system goes still further and makes it possible to use different sizes of type in the same line without difficulty in alignment. This is done by making the lining of the different sizes vary by points, so that the difference can easily be built in with leads and slugs, see page <u>14</u>. This line has *three different* **faces** and two sizes of type.

Spacing of Words and Letters. Quads and spaces are pieces of metal shorter than the type, and are used to make blank spaces between words and at the ends of lines shorter than the measure.

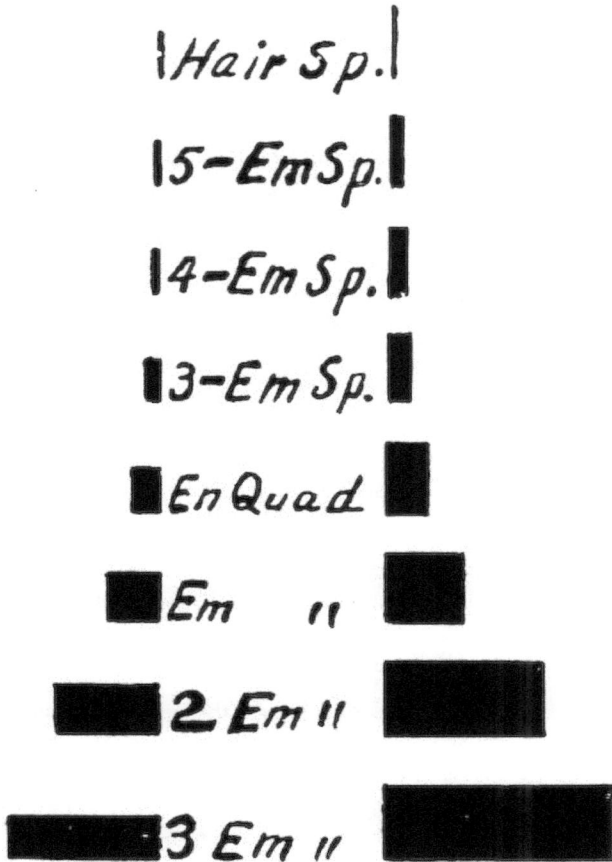

Fig. 2.

In any size of type there are four kinds of quads. Fig 2 shows the ends of the 8 and 12 point quads and spaces. An em quad is the square of the type body. The 10 point em quad is a square quad whose sides are 10 points wide. An eight point em quad is 8 points or one-ninth of an inch square.

An en quad of any size type is one-half the em quad of that size of type. A two em quad of any size type is equal to two of the square or em quads, and a three em quad is equal to three of the square or em quads laid side by side.

There are four of the thinner blanks in any size of type, known as spaces. The 3-em space is one-third of the em quad; the 4-em space one-fourth of the em quad; and the 5-em space is one-fifth of the em quad. The hair spaces are very thin spaces of copper and brass. These are very seldomly needed in general work.

The em quad must be clearly distinguished from the em pica. Every size of type has its em quad; but the em pica is simply the 12 point standard unit of measurement.

Type Font. A quantity of the same size and face of type with an assortment of the various letters and characters which are used together is called a font. Sometimes fonts are designated by the number of certain letters they contain. A font may be mentioned as having so many capital A's and so many small a's.

Type may be bought in weight or job fonts. If bought by weight, it contains capitals, small capitals, small or lower case letters, including ligatures (ff, fi, etc.), figures, marks of punctuation, spaces and quads. Twenty per cent of a weight font is made up of spaces and quads unless otherwise specified. Job fonts are small assortments of type, where only small quantities or unusual faces are needed. Such fonts do not include small capitals, spaces or quads.

Fonts or parts of fonts come from the foundry wrapped in small packages. The capitals, the small letters, and the quads and spaces come, of course, in separate packages. The letters are arranged for the most part in alphabetical order; but there is an occasional insertion of a mark of punctuation or a thin bodied letter out of regular order to fill out a line.

In taking the type from these packages, the entire face side of the mass of type is wet with soapy water. Then, beginning with the first of the alphabet, a few letters are taken at a time and put into the proper boxes of the case. This is called laying the case.

Fig. 3. NEWS CASES.

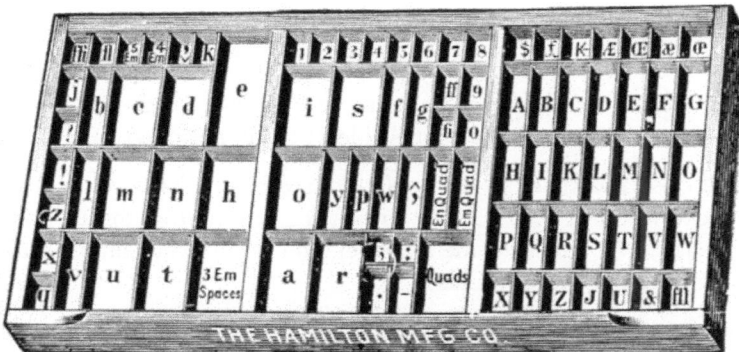

Fig. 4. JOB CASE.

Type Cases. Type cases, Figs. 3 and 4, in which type is kept are of two general kinds, news and job. News cases are in pairs, the upper and the lower case, arranged to occupy a position one above the other on top of the stand or cabinet, Fig. 5. The upper case contains the capitals, small capitals, and an assortment of signs and symbols. The lower case contains the small letters, numerals, marks of punctuation, quads and spaces. The California job case is about the size of the lower news case and fits like a drawer into a stand or cabinet. It is arranged to contain both the capitals and lower case type, but is without boxes for the small capitals. By reference to Fig. 4, it will be seen that the left side of the job case is exactly the same as the entire lower news case, except that the compartments are smaller.

Fig. 5.

The right side of the job case contains only thirty-five boxes for capitals instead of forty-nine, as in the capital side of the upper news case.

It will be observed that the capital letters are in regular order in the case with the exception of J and U. It is interesting to note that these two letters were the last to be added to the alphabet, and hence were simply placed at the last of the alphabet in the case.

In the lower case there is but little regularity of arrangement, except that the most commonly used letters occupy the most convenient and conspicuous places. The printer knows the locations of the various boxes, so that the picking out of a certain letter becomes almost purely automatic.

TYPE SETTING

In beginning to set type, the first tool the printer needs is the job stick, Fig. 6.

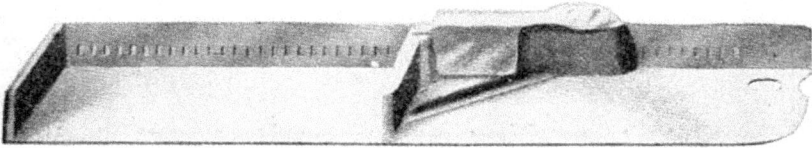

Fig. 6.

This is the receptacle into which the compositor places the type as he sets up the form, letter by letter. Sticks are made in great variety, and almost any length from six inches up. There are the simple, ungraduated stick, adjusted by the thumb screw; the marked and perforated stick for nonpareil adjustment by means of a lever, Fig. 6, and the non-adjustable stick for news or book composition.

The printer sets the stick the length of the desired line. This is done by placing into it a lead or slug, the desired length, and moving the clamp up against it tightly enough that the type will not easily fall forward, and yet loosely enough to allow the lines to be lifted from the stick without binding.

12 em 2 point Lead
Fig. 7.

Spacing of Lines. Leads (Fig. 7) are strips of metal ¾" wide, and from one to five points, inclusive, in thickness. Strips six points and thicker are called slugs. Leads and slugs are used to space between the lines of type, bearing the same relation to the lines as spaces and quads bear to the words. These strips are said to be labor saving when they are cut ready for use into definite lengths of pica or nonpareil variations. The standard lengths are from 4 to 25 ems pica. When not so cut, they are called strip.

12 em 6 point Slug
Fig. 7a.

A lead or slug generally of the thickness to give the required space between the lines, and of the length of a line, is placed in the stick, and the type is set with the top of the letter toward this lead. Then with the lead or slug in the stick and the stick in the left hand, the compositor stands upright at the case, picks out the letters and characters one at a time, and places them, nick out and face up, into the stick, beginning at the lower left hand corner. Fig. 8. As the type are put into the stick, they are held there by the thumb of the left hand. The method of holding the stick at the proper angle to prevent the type from falling out and to allow the thumb to do its work properly, is quite an art which it takes time to acquire.

Justifying lines.—The line of type reads from left to right the same as printed matter but the letters are inverted. It takes the beginner some time to accustom himself to this condition, but with practice, it becomes easy and convenient. Each word except the last in the line, is followed by a space, or a quad. In ordinary solid matter, that is matter without leads or slugs between the lines, the three-to-em spaces are used between words. But the line must come out evenly at the end without leaving a space or dividing a word improperly. This very seldom occurs in beginning work, so the young printer sets himself to the task of justifying the line, that is respacing it so as to remove the difficulty. Approved methods of spacing and justification may be found in the list of rules of composition on page 25. Great care should be observed in getting each line as nearly perfect as possible before proceeding to the next, for in this way, much trouble and annoyance in correcting proof are avoided.

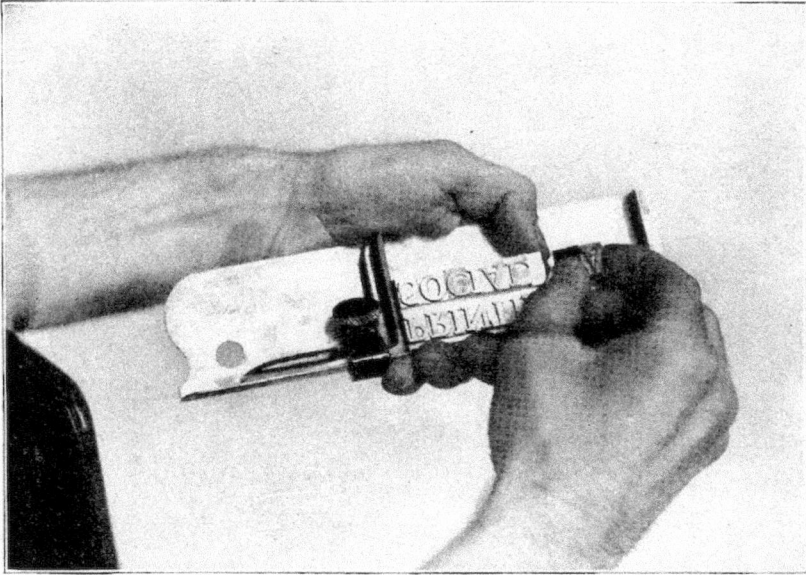

Fig. 8.

When a line has been thus finished and a lead put in above to support it, the compositor proceeds with the next line exactly as before. It is wise for the beginner to leave all the work leaded, so as to simplify the operation of removing the lines from the stick. If it is desirable, the leads or slugs may be removed after the type is emptied from the stick. If the last line of a paragraph is not a complete line, it is filled with quads and spaces, but the spaces should never be placed at the end or between the quads.

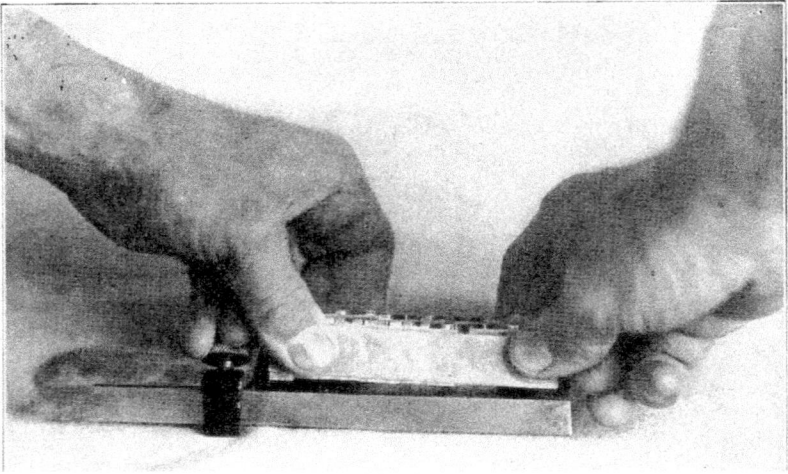

Fig. 9.

To Remove Type: The Galley. When the stick is full or nearly so, the compositor lays it down and to remove the type catches the first lead with both thumbs, and the last lead with the first finger of each hand. Fig. 9. Then he slightly raises the first line. With the remaining free fingers pressing against the ends of the lines and pushing at the same time down against the stick, he lifts the type bodily and puts it into the galley. The first line should go against the closed end and should read from the lower side of the galley up. The closed end of the galley should always be at the right as the worker stands at the case.

The galley, Fig. 10, is a kind of rectangular brass tray open at one end, into which the compositor places the lines of type on removing them from the stick. Galleys are of various sizes for different kinds of work.

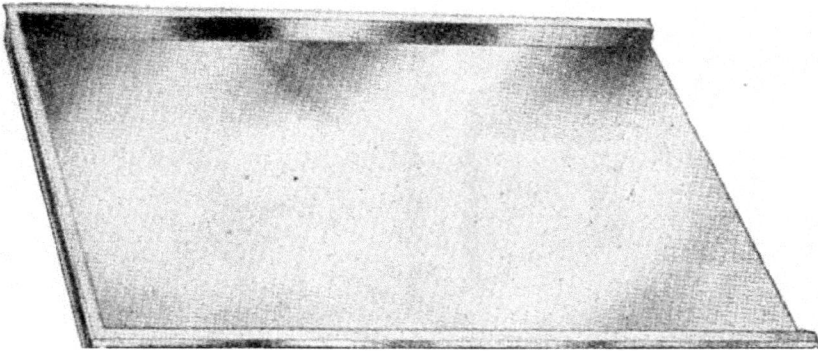

Fig. 10.

Lines and Borders: The brass rule. In case there are solid lines to be made in the printed matter, as in Fig. 11, this is done by use of the brass rule.

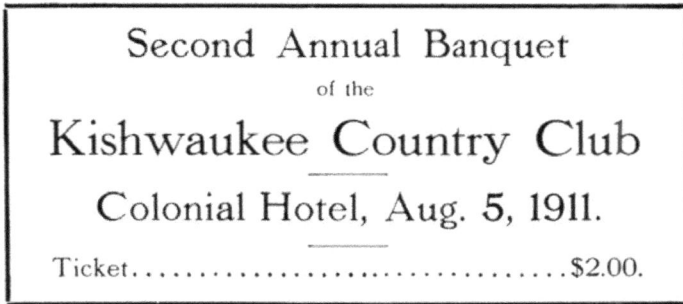

Second Annual Banquet
of the

Kishwaukee Country Club

Colonial Hotel, Aug. 5, 1911.

Ticket................................$2.00.

Fig. 11.

This, like leads, may be had either in the strip or in labor saving lengths; but unlike leads, it is type high, and is designed for the purpose of making lines, borders, etc., Fig. 12. It may be had in any thickness, but usually, a very thin face like a hair line or one point, is put on a heavier body. In such cases the rule is beveled from one or both sides and is said to be side-faced or center-faced (a and b, Fig. 12). Labor saving brass rule is made up in weight fonts, and may be had with or without mitres for the corners.

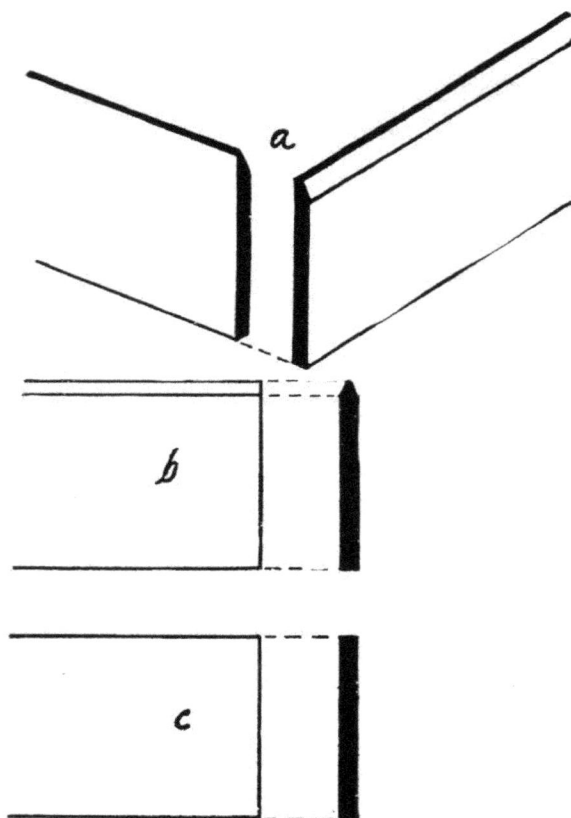

Fig. 12.

If a rule line shorter than the measure of the type line is to be made, the blank spaces at the ends of the rule are filled with leads, slugs, or quads of the same thickness as the body of the rule.

Rule for borders is put around the type form after it is finished. If the face of the rule is as thick as the body, as at c, Fig. 12, good corners are made simply by lapping one piece of rule over the end of the other piece which meets it at the corner.

If the face is thinner than the body, the rule in borders or panels must be side-faced unless there are mitres. The bevels of the side pieces of rule are turned in toward the type and those of the end pieces are turned out. The end rule laps over the ends of the side rules at the corners, as shown at a, Fig. 12.

Dotted or hyphen lines as seen in Fig. 11, are made by the use of leaders, which closely resemble quads in that they are of quad sizes. Leaders, however, are type high, and have either the dot or hyphen face—so many dots or hyphens to the em. It is not necessary to have a great variety of leader sizes, since with the point lining system, one size of leader can easily be lined with another size of type.

Spacing and Tying a Galley or Job of Type. When the compositor has finished setting the type and placed it into the galley, if it is an advertisement or small job, he proceeds to space it out by the use of leads and slugs to the required length. The form is then tied up.

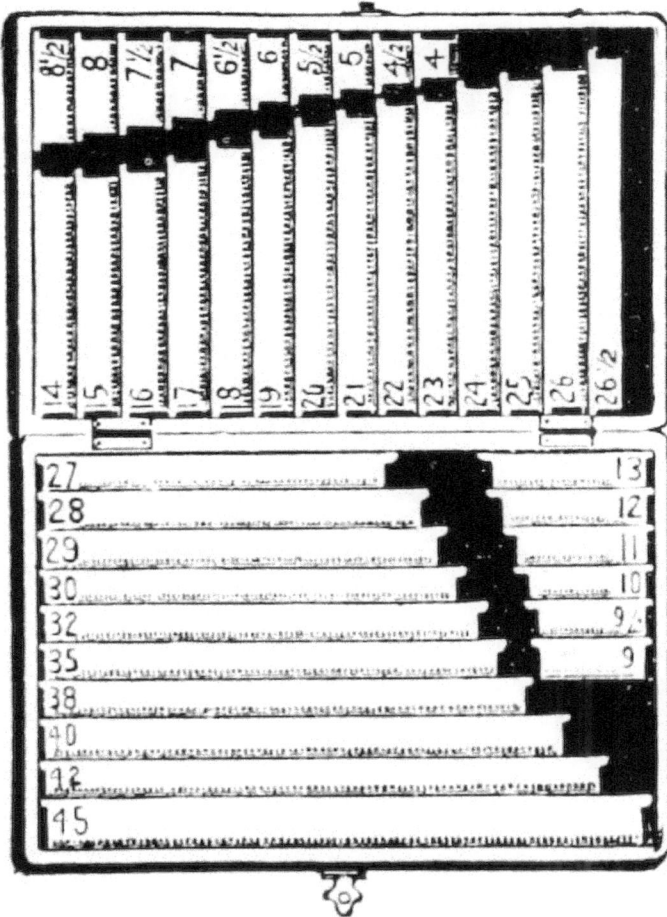

Fig. 13.

It requires considerable care and skill to tie up a mass of type properly. The form is in the lower right hand corner of the galley. The compositor takes a cotton string and beginning at the upper left hand corner, he starts to wrapping the twine around the form from left to right, drawing it taut just before turning a corner. When the starting point has been reached, he pulls the twine down across the original end thus binding it firmly against the metal. After wrapping from three to six times about the form, a loop is left in the twine, which is forced by means of a composing rule, Fig. 13, or a lead, down between the type and the strands. This leaves a small piece of the end projecting as a convenience in untying. The next step is to take a proof. The galley is laid on the stone or a table, or the form may be slid from the galley to the stone, Fig. 18.

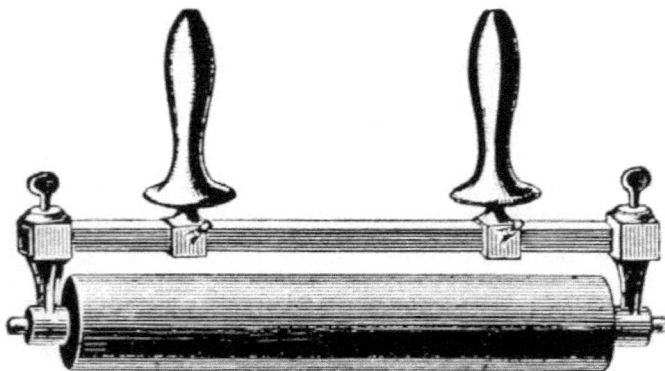

Fig. 14.

Fig. 15.

Taking a Proof. When the tied form has been placed upon the stone or proof press, it is inked by rolling a small rubber roller (Fig. 14) over it, the roller having been first well inked by rolling it over an inked piece of marble, slate or glass. Then the type is covered with a moist paper, the sponged side up, or a regular proof paper. If there is no proof press the proof planer, a smooth faced block of hard wood, with face covered with felt, Fig. 15, is laid on the top of the paper, and tapped squarely and firmly with the mallet.

If the proof planer does not cover the form, its position is changed and the mallet used again. The impression left on the paper is the first proof. See proof marks, page 27. In school, it is wise to have the pupils read their own proofs.

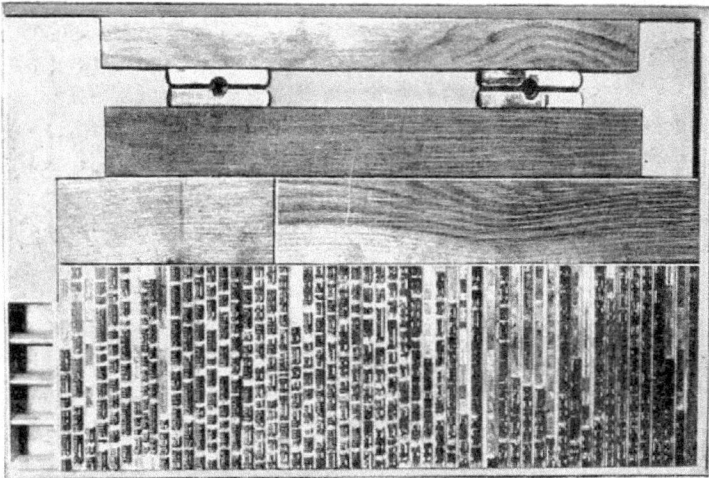

Fig. 16.

To correct a galley. Then with the marked proof before him, the compositor proceeds to correct. If only slight changes are to be made, such as turning an inverted letter or taking out a capital and putting in a lower case letter, such changes may be made without lifting the type into the stick. Often lines or words are transposed, or omissions or repetitions are discovered. Such errors necessitate respacing and overrunning, by which is meant the going over several lines respacing them and crowding a word out of one line into another in order to correct an error. In such cases, it is well to lift out into the stick, the lines involved. In the matter of taking out a letter, it is necessary only to press lightly at both ends of the line with the thumb and finger of one hand, raising the line about half way out of the form, and with the other hand to remove the desired letter and allow the line to slide back into its original position. Bodkins and tweezers are dangerous and useless instruments in most instances. After the changes indicated in the first proof have been made, a second proof is taken to make sure that all corrections have been made, and that no new errors have crept in. This proof should be submitted to the instructor for approval. It may be necessary to make a number of proofs before a perfect impression is gotten. In case of a sufficient quantity of matter to necessitate its division into pages or columns, the proof is taken in the galley without tying up, Fig. 16. The form is locked tightly in the galley by means of furniture and quoins, Fig. 16. This is somewhat like the lockup described on page 32, except that furniture is placed only on one side of the mass of type.

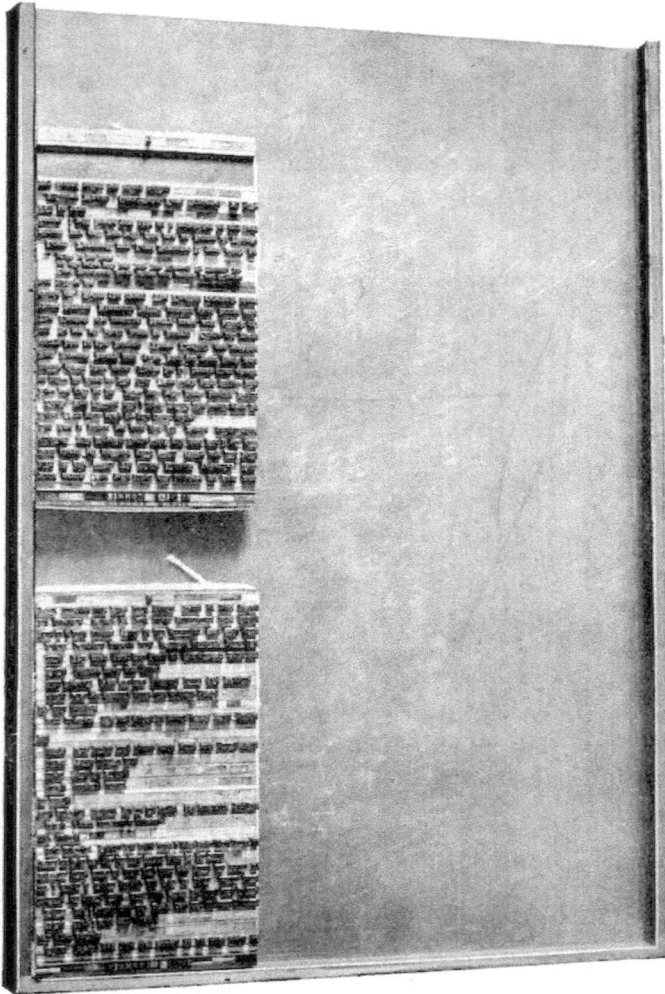

Fig. 17.

Making up. When the corrections are made, the matter is properly divided, the page numbers and headings are placed, and the pages or columns are tied up. This process is called making up. Fig. 17. When the printer begins to make up, he has before him a long mass of type, as at Fig. 16. The length of the page is determined. It includes the page number, the running head, if there be one, and a nonpareil, or six point, slug at each end.

A page 18 ems wide might properly be 30 ems long. In this case, the measure would be 31 ems and a 31 em reglet, (see furniture page 31) answers well for a measure, as will any long piece of furniture on which the desired length may be marked. An accurate ruler may be used to advantage. The length of the first page is usually less than the full measure and is somewhat arbitrarily determined. It is generally sunken about one-fourth of the page. After this page is tied up and moved aside, the page number, the running head and the slug are added to the remaining column of type and the measure applied for the next page. This is repeated until the final page is reached, which is usually somewhat less than the full measure.

RULES OF COMPOSITION

1. Spacing between words should appear as nearly uniform as possible, not only throughout the line but throughout the entire piece of work.

2. For solid, or unleaded matter, the em quad is used to indent the paragraph, and to follow a period except at the end of a line; the 3 to em space, between words in the absence of marks of punctuation other than the comma; the en quad, after a semi-colon and also after a colon when followed by a lower case letter, but when followed by a capital letter, the space should be slightly larger, perhaps two 3 to em spaces.

3. The indentation and spaces between words should vary according to the spaces between the lines. In case of two point leaded matter, the en quad should be used instead of the 3 to em space and other spaces should be correspondingly larger.

4. In justifying a line after the spacing has been done *according* to the above rules, spaces may be increased at kern letters, f, y, etc., between long words, and after semi-colons and colons; or reduced at slanting letters, at commas, and at the sides of small words. Spaces should be the same on both sides of very small words, and there should never be a greater variation in the spacing between ordinary words than the difference between an en quad and a 3 to em space.

5. Type should stand squarely on foot.

6. Divisions of words at the ends of the lines should be avoided wherever possible but when divided, the proper division of syllables should always be made.

7. Avoid dividing short words, or dividing words by cutting off short syllables at the first or last.

8. Do not loosen the clamp of the stick in order to make it possible to insert a space.

9. When in doubt about spelling, punctuation, capitalization, or syllabication, consult authority.

10. Save endless time and trouble by producing a clean proof the first time.

11. In making up, it is good form to have the first and last lines of a page full lines. So it is best not to have a paragraph begin with the first line or end with the last line of a page.

PROOF MARKS

l.c. Change to LOWER CASE.

s.c. Change to SMALL CAPITALS.

caps. Change to capitals.

rom. Change to *roman,*

ital. Change to italic.

bold Change to bold face.

Put in hyphen.

Turn inverted letter.

Take out.

stet Leave or reinstate part ~~crossed~~ out.

w.f. Wrong font.

Indent line.

\# Put space between words.

Start new paragraph.

Move to the left.

Move to the right.

Raise up letters or words.

Bring letters down in line.

V∧ Make spaces uniform.

X Broken or imperfect letter.

? Question for author.

Close up space.

out-copy Part of copy omitted.

⊙ ⋏ Period and comma.

Apostrophe.

tr. Transpose or letters words.

IMPOSITION

Imposition is the arranging of the type masses in proper order on the stone, and the fastening of them into the chase.

Fig. 18.—BACK VIEW.

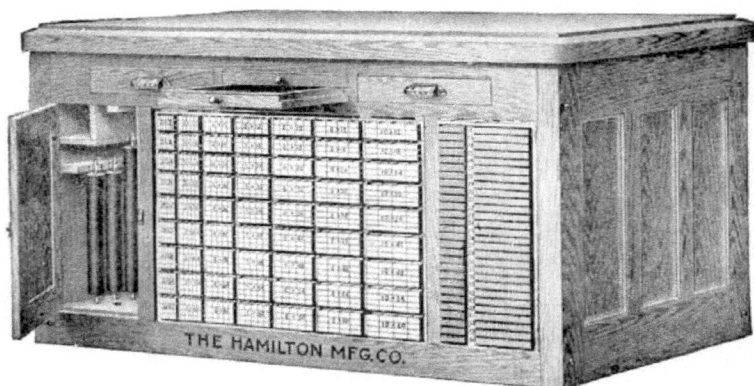

Fig. 18.—FRONT VIEW.

The imposing stone, Fig. 18, is a smooth marble slab on which the forms are placed for locking up ready for the press. The stone may be laid upon a box, bench or table, but both stands and cabinets are made for this purpose. It is properly bedded in its "coffin" by placing putty along the edges of the bed and along any cross supports which may run under the stone. Then when the stone is placed into this receptacle, it remains solid and level and free from strain. It should project a short distance above the frame of the bed in order to render easy the removal of the forms to and from the galley.

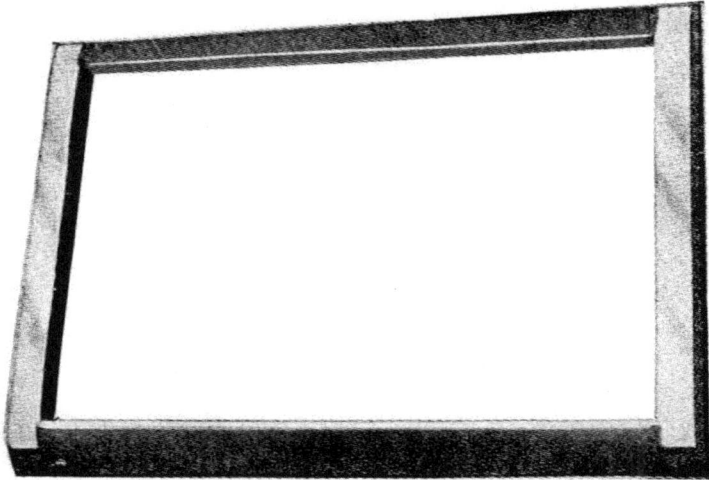

Fig. 19.

The chase, Fig. 19, is a steel or cast-iron frame, into which the forms are locked to be put into the press. The size of a press is based upon the inside dimensions of the chase. A 10 × 15 press is one that accommodates a 10 × 15 chase. The skeleton chase is a steel chase with a very narrow frame. This makes the inside considerably larger. A skeleton chase for a 10 × 15 press is practically 11 × 16, making a clear gain of almost an inch each way.

When the type has been proofed, corrected, made up, and tied, the form is slipped from the galley to the stone, and is then ready for the lockup, Fig. 20.

Fig. 20.

A chase is put upon the stone in such a position as to form a frame about the type, which as a rule should occupy the central part of the space enclosed by the frame. A roller supporter, a, Fig. 20, is placed in each end of the chase and pieces of furniture are built out solidly from the type form to one side and one end of the chase.

Fig. 21.

Furniture, Fig. 21, and b, c, Fig. 20, is the name given to pieces of wood and metal, which are used to build around the forms in the process of locking them into the chase. Furniture varies by the em in width and by 5 to 10 ems in length when cut labor saving. Metal furniture is more modern and makes possible more accurate work; but for beginners, it has its disadvantages. The metal is soft and of considerable weight, making heavier forms; and if a piece is dropped upon the stone or even upon the floor, which frequently happens, it probably has a corner or an edge battered. In the lockup, occasionally this small defect may cause the "pi" of the whole form. Reglets are a kind of wood furniture similar in size and use to leads and slugs but are largely used as furniture in locking up forms. In leaded forms which have to be kept for sometime, reglets are substituted for the leads and slugs. They are very much cheaper, and they relieve the necessity for large quantities of the more expensive leads and slugs. Wood furniture, which comes by the case or by number of pieces, is cheap, durable, not easily injured, and on the whole, quite satisfactory for school use. A small amount of metal furniture, which is sold by weight, is desirable in every printshop.

When the furniture has been built in at one side and one end of the form as indicated above, quoins are placed at the other side and the other end about midway between the type and the chase.

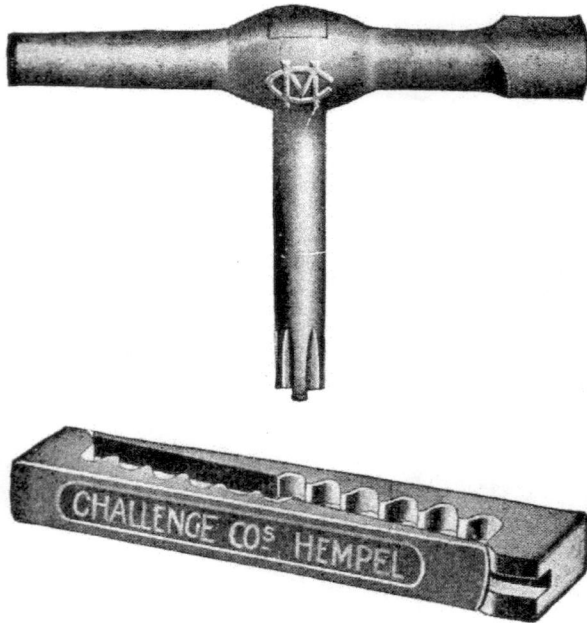

Fig. 22.

Quoins, Fig. 22, are devices for locking the forms into the chases. There are two chief kinds, one consisting of two separate wedge shaped pieces of hard metal with notched sides, which by the use of a key are made to slide in opposite directions against each other. The danger of these quoins in the hands of schoolboys is that, not realizing how easily good forms are held, they persist in trying to screw the quoin to the last notch, frequently endangering the chase and ruining the quoins. The other kind is constructed of two pieces of metal joined by springs and opened by the use of a key operating a nut which, after a slight expansion of the quoin, releases its hold and allows the parts to spring back together. This quoin is safe for the form and for the chase, and is itself not battered in the process of locking up.

After the quoins have been put into proper position, pieces of furniture are fitted in on both sides of the quoins.

The pieces of furniture are usually a little longer than the sides of the form against which they fit. They are always placed around the form in such a way that they can not bind against each other so as to prevent the pressure from striking the type squarely, Fig. 20.

With the key, Fig. 22, the quoins are very slightly and uniformly tightened. Then the planer is used.

Fig. 23.

The planer, Fig. 23, is a smooth faced block of hard wood similar to the proof planer, but is usually smaller and not covered with felt. This is laid on the face of the form on the stone and tapped lightly with a mallet, in order to make sure that the faces of all the type are at the same level—no letters projecting so as to be broken or to injure the rollers, or, at best, to ruin the impressions.

After this, the printer tightens the quoins gradually, giving a slight turn to each quoin in succession. There is danger of the beginner's getting the lockup too tight, causing the form to spring up from the stone and the chase to spring and even to break. If the composition is good and the furniture is properly placed, it does not require a very tight lockup to hold. Before removing the chase from the stone, the lockup should be tested by raising one side of the chase very slightly and tapping the furniture to see if any of the type are loose. If the form holds, it is ready for the press.

Forms for Four and More Pages. When there are a number of pages instead of one to be dealt with, the imposition is considerably more complicated.

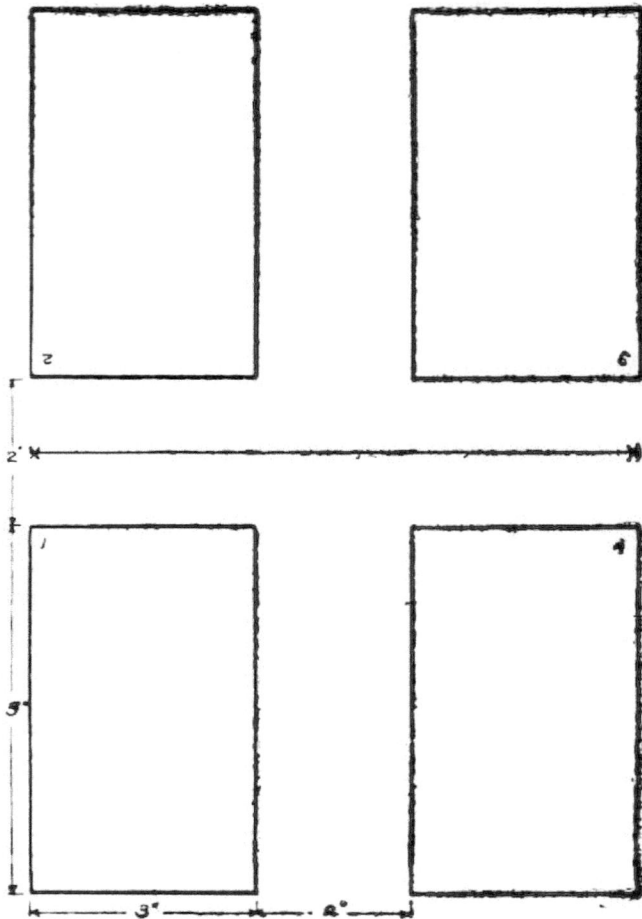

Fig. 24.

Any piece of printing of four or more pages has an outside and an inside section. Page one and all the pages that are printed on the same side of the paper with it constitute the outside section. Page two and all the pages that are printed on the same side with it are the inside section. A four page printed sheet is called a sheet folio. The best way to handle such a four page form is by the work-and-turn method, provided the press is large enough to accommodate the four pages at one time. By this method, the pages are arranged as in Fig. 24. Note that in this form as in any other outside form, page one is at the lower left hand corner with the foot of the page toward the printer. Margins are determined by measuring from the front of type pages one and two the width of the page plus twice the desired margin to the backs of pages three and four. Then the length of the page plus twice the margin is measured from the foot of pages one and four to the head of pages two and three.

In this case, the stock is cut double the length of the finished job. When it has been printed on one side, and the ink has dried, it is turned and given the same impression on the other side. Of course, in printing this second side, care must be taken to reverse the paper so that pages two and three back up one and four at one end, and one and four back up two and three at the other end. When the ink of this impression is dry, the sheet is cut at line XX making two complete folios from one sheet.

With school boys working on a small press, the four pages are often handled in two separate forms of two pages each.

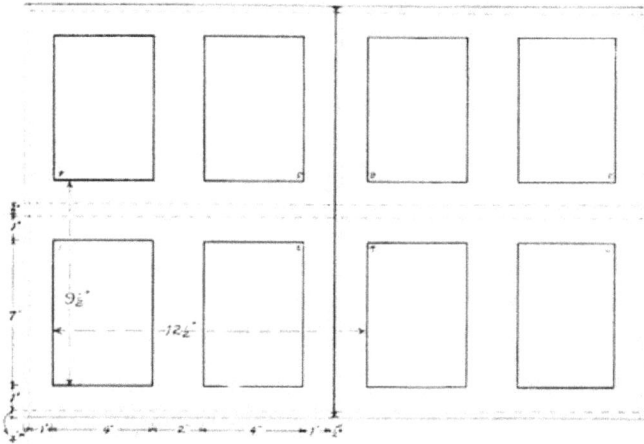

Fig. 25.

When so divided, each pair may be imposed in exactly the same order as in the four page form. In this case the paper is cut to exact size and pages one and four are printed on one side. When the ink dries, it is run through the press again and pages two and three are printed on the other side, completing the work.

An eight page form, or a sheet quarto, for a sufficiently large press, may be imposed after the work-and-turn method as in the case of the four page form. The numbered rectangles in Fig. 25 show the arrangement of pages in the work-and-turn method of imposing an eight page form. It will be observed that pages in the outside section of an eight page form are in the same order as those of a four page form. For a press that can accommodate only four pages, the inside and outside sections are imposed exactly in the same order as in Fig. 25, but are used as separate forms.

When we undertake the imposition of an eight page job, we meet the problem of margin for trim, which has not been encountered in the previous forms. In an eight page piece of work, there must be two folds and since the sheets are folded after they are printed and before they are cut, it is evident that some allowance must be made for trimming the fold at the top of the pages. Since in folding, the edges are probably not even, it is necessary to trim them also. Thus it is clear that allowance must be made for trim around each pair of leaves. Fig. 25 represents a half sheet of standard 25×38 paper laid on the eight page form imposed by the work-and-turn method. The line XX indicates where the printed half sheet is cut before folding. The dotted lines indicate the margins allowed for trim after folding. The method of measuring for the imposition is as follows: Suppose the type pages to be four by seven inches and centered in the pages, and the margin, after trim, to be one inch all around each page.

It is apparent then that the backs of type pages 8 and 5 are two inches from the backs of pages 1 and 4. The location of pages 7 and 6 is determined by measuring half the length of the half sheet, or 12½ inches in this case, from the front edges of type pages 1 and 4. The distance then from 8 to 7 and from 5 to 6 is 2½ inches or 15 ems pica, making ½ inch for trim. One-half of 19 inches, or the other dimension of the half sheet, measured from the foot of type page 1 to the head of 4, places the distance of 2½ inches between 1 and 4. This allows ½ inch here also for trim.

In this work, some prefer simply to fold the paper and use it for measurement, but in any case when the margins are determined, they are built in with appropriate furniture and the form is locked up. It is well to remember that, viewed from the foot of the pages in a form, odd numbered pages are always at the left of even numbered pages.

In most of the work of this character, the pages are so large that only two may be accommodated by a small press. In this case, the eight pages are imposed in pairs as follows: One and eight, two and seven, three and six, and four and five. It will be observed that the sum of the page numbers of any pair is always one greater than the whole number of pages.

PRESSWORK

Fig. 26.

The first thing in the matter of handling a press, Fig. 26, is to have a clear idea in mind as to the method of its operation; the next is to make sure that the press is well oiled, well cleaned and the bed and platen clean of all grit, paper, gauge pins, quadrats, etc.

The throw off, a, Fig. 26, is a lever by use of which the press can be prevented from printing. This should always be in such position as to hold the platen, b, away from the bed, c, until the press is ready for an impression.

An essential part of the press which needs to be mentioned separately is the rollers, d.

They are a kind of rubbery composition moulded around steel rods or cores; and when placed on the press, they distribute the ink over the plate, e, and carry it down upon the type. Of course, they are soft and pliable and need proper attention to keep them so. There are summer rollers and winter rollers and neither can be used to advantage out of season. Winter rollers become too soft for summer, while the reverse is true of summer rollers used in winter. Seventy degrees is about the right temperature to insure the proper working of rollers. When they become permanently hard enough to retain, for a considerable time, the type impressions, rollers are said to be dead. Much can be told about rollers by observing the color and the shine of the surface. A dead roller has a dead, lusterless surface. When rollers are worn out, they are simply sent to the factory where the old composition is removed and new composition molded upon the same cores. The chief constituents of rollers are molasses, glycerine and glue.

Make-ready. In preparing the make-ready, a hard surfaced piece of pressboard is placed on the platen. On top of this, should be from three to five pieces of book paper for "packing," covered finally with a "drawsheet" of tough manila. Now the press is inked by putting upon the plate, e, a small quantity of ink and allowing the press to run until the rollers have thoroughly distributed it over the plate. Then the form is put into the press at c, and care is used to see that the grippers, f, are properly adjusted so that they do not strike the form and at the same time, are not far enough out to strike the roller supporters. In case of interference of grippers, one or both may be removed. When everything is ready, an impression is taken on the draw sheet and is examined to see if any type are high, or to discover and correct any other defect. Then the lower clamp, g, is loosened and while the draw sheet is thrown back, an impression is taken on the top sheet of the packing. If a portion of the impression is indistinct, a thin piece of paper is pasted upon the indistinct parts to give them a slightly heavier impression. This is known as the overlay. In patching up the make-ready in this manner, it is very important that the overlay shall not reach beyond the parts which need building up. If an indistinctness in an impression is due to worn type or a low cut, it may be remedied by an underlay. This is the pasting of bits of paper or cardboard to the foot of the type, or to the back of the cut. In case a portion shows too heavy an impression, that particular part is cut out of the top sheet of the packing. Then the draw sheet is clamped down again and a device is arranged for holding the stock for printing.

Fig. 27.

For locating the positions of the gauge pins, Fig. 27, or quadrats, the stock is laid straight across the impression allowing the ends to project equally over the ends of the impression, and with a sharp pencil, a mark is made on the draw sheet along the left end of the stock. Then the stock is slipped down across the impression in such a way as to allow the edges of the stock to project the distance of the desired margins above and below the impression on the drawsheet. A mark is then placed along the lower edge of the stock. The gauge pins or quads are placed on these two lines, two on the horizontal and one on the vertical, in such a position as will best hold the stock on the platen. If quads are used, they are glued to the drawsheet. It usually takes several impressions on the cut stock to get a perfect adjustment. In order to prevent the stock from being lifted from the platen by the ink, a small cord is tied about the ends of the grippers in such a position as that it strikes the stock above the impression of the type.

Constant care must be exercised to keep the grippers from getting in the way of the roller supporters and causing considerable injury.

The pupils in school begin operating the press very slowly and by foot power. The process of feeding is largely a matter of cultivating a certain ambidexterity and a rhythmic movement of the hands, the right to place the blank sheet upon the platen, and the left to remove it after it is printed. Great care must be taken to avoid soiling the stock or smearing the ink on removing the freshly printed sheets. As skill is acquired, speed should be increased. Finally the boys are able safely to feed a motor driven press. When the matter is printed, it is carefully scattered over the letter boards, table, or shelves to dry, and the chase is removed to the stone.

CLEANING AND DISTRIBUTING

After finishing the job of printing proper, there are still some very important things to do. The form must be cleaned, the ink thoroughly removed from the press, and the type thrown back into the proper cases, or distributed.

The form is cleaned by going over the type, first with a cotton cloth moistened with benzine, and following with a bristle brush. The press also must be washed, that is the ink must be removed from the plate and the rollers. With cotton rags or waste moistened with benzine, the ink is wiped off the plate. Then the rollers are run upon the plate, and with the cloth still further moistened with benzine, the rollers are carefully gone over and all the ink removed. The rollers are then run down from the plate, which is wiped clean and dry. In case waste is used in cleaning the rollers, it should be wrapped inside of a cloth to prevent threads and lint from adhering to them. To the inexperienced, this matter of cleaning the press, gives the impression of a long, tedious and dirty task. It proves to be quite an interesting demonstration for the instructor to wash the press clean, and come through the process in three minutes with hands scarcely soiled. There grows up somewhat of a rivalry among the groups or individuals to see which can wash the press in the shortest time and with the least muss. In leaving the press, this caution should always be kept in mind; never allow the rollers to remain on the plate or on a form in the press. Rags that have become saturated with benzine and ink should be burned or kept in a closed can.

It is the practice with a great many good printers to leave the ink on the press over night, after thoroughly oiling it with lubricating oil. By thus leaving the rollers covered with this soft, oily coat, the composition is protected from the drying and hardening effects of the air. Of course there are inks which harden in spite of the oil, such as gilts, bronzes, bronze blues, reds, etc. Such inks should not be left on the press longer than necessary.

The next morning, the oily ink is easily removed with a dry cloth. Sometimes, it is well to follow up with a cloth slightly moistened with benzine.

In case ink has been permitted to harden on the rollers, it may be removed by taking the rollers from the press, washing them with moderately strong lye, using a printer's scrub brush. After the ink is removed, the rollers are thoroughly rinsed in water.

When type has been allowed to remain without the ink having been cleaned off, and the ink has hardened and cemented the type together, it may be loosened and cleaned with lye. Make a strong solution of lye and saturate the mass of type with it. Rub the lye in thoroughly with the scrub brush, leave the lye on the type for two hours and then rinse in water. Keep repeating this process until the type is loosened and cleaned.

When a form has been used and is no longer needed, it is called dead matter and is ready for distribution. To prepare the type for distribution, a sponge is saturated with soapy water and the top of the form thoroughly wet, so that the water makes its way down into the small crevices between the type. If the form is put into a galley, it is placed in the same position as for tying up. Then the printer takes upon a slug the last two, three, or four lines and holds them in his left hand as in Fig. 28, so that the lines occupy the same position as when in the stick. With the right hand, he picks up one or more words from the right end of the top line. Standing before his case in the same position as when setting type, he spells the words back into the case. It is very important that type be properly distributed, that the letters, characters, and spaces be put into their proper boxes. This is interesting work, and beginners delight in it; besides, it is a work in which considerable skill can quite readily be acquired.

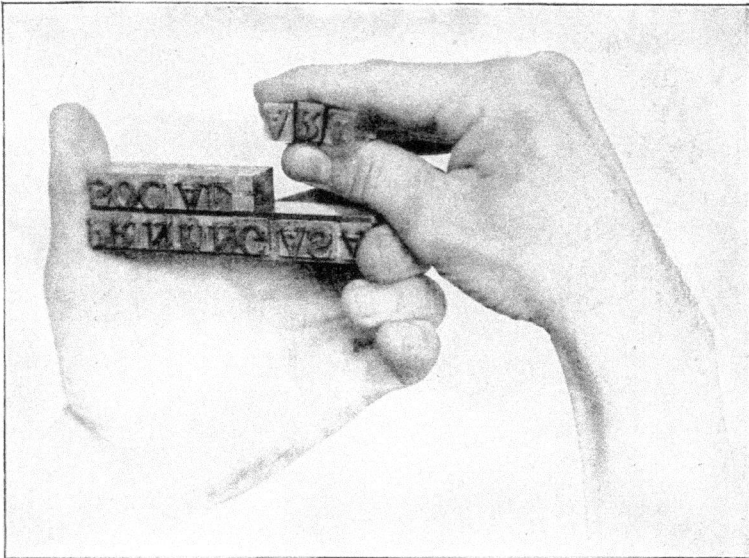

Fig. 28.

The proper time to rescue a letter from the floor or from a wrong box into which it has been dropped, is immediately after it has been so misplaced. Leads, slugs, furniture, and rule should be put at once in proper positions into their respective places.

WHAT TO PRINT AND HOW TO PROCEED

In discussing the matter of the proper printing for the public schools, let us not forget this general proposition, i. e., that the claim of printing to a place as a school art must rest upon its force as an educational factor and not upon the fact that, by a species of child labor, money may be made or saved.

There may be done some work of a commercial nature, of course, as in any kind of so-called industrial work, and thereby money be saved for the institution or the community. But the fact that some of the work results in financial gain or saving is incidental, although it may help to add interest and reality to the work. However, the work of the school print shop should be largely such as, in the absence of the school shop, would not be printed.

School printing may be grouped loosely into three classes:

1. Material whose content appeals to the pupils and whose merit justifies permanent form. It is always a happy condition when the matter which we ask the boys and girls to print appeals to them on its own merit as something that deserves to be perpetuated. The book idea presupposes permanency of content. So the book, printed and bound by the pupils and containing their favorite selections, makes a strong appeal. Literature classes collect ballads, lyrics, and other forms of literature for such work. Books of ballads suited to the various grades might profitably be prepared. The broadsheet idea may be taken advantage of to popularize national airs, patriotic songs, crisp maxims, rare bits of humor, etc.

2. Such temporary material as connects intimately with the school work and does a genuine service. An abundance of valuable material may be found in connection with elementary reading, nature study, geography, gardening, constructive work, etc. Stories relating to these subjects and written by the children may be printed and furnished to the children for reading matter. The development of dramatization in the schools offers material for the printshop. A story like "Treasure Island" or "Kinmont Willie" is read by the boys and girls, who set themselves to the task of putting it into dramatic form. Pupils take up the work of printing such a production with the greatest of interest whether it is the work of their own or of another class. The school paper is a valuable thing from every point of view. Spelling lists, binders' notes inserted in rebound books, programs of school entertainments, Xmas and Easter cards, etc., come under this second division.

3. This class includes such work as would ordinarily be sent to the commercial printer. Letter heads, office blanks, report cards, business notices, official announcements, etc., come under this head. Some of this can be handled to the profit of both the boys and the school and without injustice to the commercial printer.

In beginning printing with a class, it is believed to be best to take advantage of the wide-eyed curiosity and intense interest of the pupils, simply to make them familiar with the locations of the various parts of the equipment and the names of the various tools of the printer. Just the pointing out and reciting of the names of the leads, slugs, furniture, etc., are sufficient to hold the rapt attention of the class.

During the early period is a good time for investigations by the pupils as to the origin and development of printing, the story of movable type, the evolution of the press, the relation of printing to progress, etc. This plan of having the pupils get as much relevant information as possible concerning their new activity, under the impulse of this first enthusiasm, proves to be an effective method of teaching as well as valuable and timely work for the boys and girls. The same eagerness to become familiar with the work makes the lay of the cases an easy matter to get before the class. Almost without exception the boys ask for the privilege of making individual diagrams of the cases, for pocket reference. The very irregularity and confusion of the lower case somehow appeal to the boys, and they take great pride in mastering what seems at first glance almost a puzzle.

The explanation that j and u were the last letters added to the alphabet and that they occupy positions in the capital case corresponding to the time of their additions, makes the lay of the capital case easy to remember.

Considerable time may well be devoted to just this kind of work.

In familiarizing themselves with the case, the pupils may well begin the use of the job stick and the practice of properly holding it, by the use of large type, in setting up their names and such simple matter as they care to attempt, putting the type back again into the proper boxes. When simple composition is begun, it is thought best that each piece of work should run through the typical processes, setting up the type, emptying the stick, proofing, correcting, tying up, removing to the stone, locking up, and printing. The presswork for these first efforts may be done by the teacher by way of demonstrations, so that the pupils become familiar with the methods of handling a press.

The class should be kept for a considerable time on such work as labels, name cards, spelling lists, etc., gradually working into the longer compositions of plain, straight matter.

When it comes to the larger jobs, one piece of work may be divided among several pupils or even the whole class.

Of course, in all this work, there must be constant reference and attention to the various rules of composition, such as justification, spacing, margins, etc.

As the class advances, it is well to have each boy do a little press work by himself. He will prepare the make-ready, which the instructor has previously demonstrated, ink the press, set the gauge pins, and run off the job, under the close scrutiny of the teacher. In handling jobs of two or more pages, the pupils have experience in proofing, making up the matter into page forms, and of imposing or locking it up. It is well to have the list of proof marks conspicuously on the board and to insist upon the pupils' use of them in a correct and intelligent way.

At the close of the eighth year and in the high school, the handling of cuts, tabular work, and the more difficult processes all along the line is expected.

Not only must the boys use the cuts in printing but they ought to make the wood cuts, zinc etchings, and copper plates as frequently as possible from designs and illustrations prepared by themselves.

During the work in printing, the teacher should not overlook or neglect any illustrative material that may be available, and which may be of value in setting standards, arousing ambitions, and offering suggestions for improvement. Visits to commercial print shops are an excellent thing from the standpoint of all these considerations. In studying the arrangements of the parts of a broken page, or of an advertisement, it has proved interesting and profitable to cut out the parts of the printed matter collected for study, and to reassemble them by pasting them to another page. The variety in the matter of margins, spacing, and grouping that can be had by such a treatment, is often really surprising. Then when there are added the possibilities of different sizes and kinds of type, the colors of ink, and the colors and textures of paper, the effects that may be produced are without limit.

METHOD OF TEACHING THE LOWER CASE

Each boy has a case before him. The class is told that there are three little groups of letters to be learned first: *ar, is, jk*. These groups are learned first, because they are not consecutive and do not readily fall into the grouping which is to follow.

After these first groups have been fixed in the mind, it is explained that the left half of the lower case is made up, for the most part, of groups of letters which are consecutive in the alphabet. These groups are: *bcde, lmn (h) o, tuv*. Besides *jk* on the left side there is another nonconsecutive group, *qxz*. These groups are repeatedly pointed out during the explanation. When we come to the group *lmn (h) o*, we say "*lmn* over *h* to *o*."

Beginning with *a*, the class repeats several times these groups: *bcde, lmn (h) o, tuv, qxz*. Then it is pointed out that there are only two groups remaining, and that they are on the right hand side of the case. They are *fg* and *ypw*.

When the boys have located the groups a few times, they are tested on the entire alphabet in order. They begin, *a, bcde, fg*, and then they remember the "over *h* to *o*" expression, which locates *h* for them. The next letters, *i* and *jk*, are in the first groups learned and hence are easily recalled. Then follows the group *lmno*. If they do not readily locate *p*, the group *ypw* is repeated by the teacher. The letter *q* is in the corner group, *qxz*, *r* is in the first group learned, *ar*, and *s* is in the second group learned, *is*. The next letters, *tuv*, are in a group by themselves, and the remaining letters of the alphabet, *w, x, y, z*, are in the two remaining groups, *ypw* and *qxz*.

If at any time, a boy cannot locate a letter, he can be immediately assisted if the teacher will simply repeat the group in which the letter is to be found. For instance, if he cannot find *x*, the teacher should simply say "qxz."

The location of quads, spaces, numerals, and "points" is only a matter of a short time, and may be learned at the time the letter boxes are learned, but can just as well be taught when an explanation of the quads and spaces is made.

It will be observed that by this plan, instead of learning the positions of twenty-six separate boxes, the boys learn the positions of the following nine groups: *ar, is, jk, bcde, lmn (h) o, tuv, qxz, fg, ypw*, which include the twenty-six.

WOOD CUTS AND METAL PLATES

The making of wood cuts and metal plate etchings has proved one of the greatest sources of interest and educational profit to the boys and girls. It vitalizes and lends motive to design and illustration, it requires very little equipment and is a perfectly feasible scheme even for the seventh and eighth grades.

It is perhaps as well to illustrate the idea with a concrete problem. A book is being made for instance, by each pupil. He plans a cover design, a bookplate or an illustration. After the design or illustration is carefully worked out, it is traced in reverse by means of carbon paper upon a piece of wood, copper, or zinc. If it is to be a wood cut, the block is squared up to the proper thickness, about seven-eights of an inch. Birch, maple, and black walnut have proved very satisfactory for this work. Of course, in commercial work, boxwood is extensively used and the design cut on the end grain; but it is very satisfactory and much easier for the school work, to cut the figure on the side of a piece of ordinary board. With a small veining tool, such as is used in wood carving, the design is outlined, care being taken to leave the edges of the parts to be left in relief sharp and distinct. Then with a small gouge, chisel or knife, the background is cut away to the depth of about one-sixteenth of an inch. No care need be taken to make the background smooth.

Of course, the open grained woods do not give a solid, uniform impression. This is not at all objectionable as one may see by examining the wood cuts of the old masters. However, if a dense impression is desired, this experiment has been tried with good results: After the design is cut, the face of the block is gone over with a heavy coat of thick woodfiller. When the filler is dry, it is carefully scraped from the face of the design. By this simple method, a dense, clear, and uniform impression is made possible.

If it is to be a metal plate, the pupil simply takes a thick, smooth piece of copper or zinc, traces the design, and with a water color brush, he paints with asphaltum varnish the parts of the design to be left in relief. The back of the metal plate is also covered with a thin coat of the varnish. Careful examination is made to see whether air bubbles have caused small holes in the varnish, or anything else has caused any portion of the design to be left uncovered. When dry, the acid bath is prepared. Commercial nitric acid is the safest solution. It is diluted by adding about an equal volume of water to it, making it from 15% to 20% strong. The diluted acid is poured into a glass or porcelain tray and the plate put into it. If the acid can be kept moving by frequently rocking the tray, the etching will be very materially hastened. It takes from three to five hours to etch deeply a piece of copper, depending upon the strength and amount of the solution and the amount of exposed surface to be eaten away. If large surfaces are to be etched, quite a large quantity of acid is desirable, or else a changing or strengthening of the solution during the process. As soon as the acid becomes somewhat burdened with the metal, it ceases to act at all freely, and even begins to deposit a blue nitrate upon the metal. In such a case, it is best to put the plate into a fresh solution.

Fig. 29.

Care must be taken that the acid is not too strong, as the heat generated by its rapid action softens the varnish and lets the acid under to play havoc with the design. Numerous bubbles and yellow-green fumes indicate that the acid should be weakened by the addition of a small quantity of water.

By observing the progress of the etching occasionally, it can be told when the proper depth has been reached. Then the plate is heated sufficiently to soften the varnish, soaked in kerosene or turpentine, and rubbed clean with a cloth. Or the warm varnish can be removed by simply saturating the cloth with kerosene, turpentine, or benzine and rubbing over it.

A block of wood is then prepared for a base so that the mounted plate is slightly less in thickness than the height of the type. Then with a punch or a small drill, holes are put into the lower, or background, part of the metal. Through these holes the plate is fastened to the block by small tacks or escutcheon pins, the heads being sunken below the surface of the background. Large surfaces of background should be sawed out before the metal is mounted upon the block. When the cut is used in printing, it is brought up to the proper height by the underlaying of paper or cardboard.

This work is used extensively in connection with such work as cards and programs for Xmas, Thanksgiving, Easter and other special occasions. Fig. 29.

THE EQUIPMENT—ITS SELECTION
AND COST

In planning an equipment for a print shop, as for any other shop, the more specific the conditions and limitations under which one is placed, the more intelligently one can go about the undertaking. In the first place, the following things should be as definitely decided upon as possible:

1. The grade and number of pupils who are going to handle the equipment.

2. The nature of the work anticipated.

3. Amount of money to be expended.

This is only another way of saying that a school printshop must meet school conditions. There are a number of points in which the school print shop differs materially from the commercial job shop. The number that must be kept at work is an illustrative point.

From the standpoint of durability and of quality of the work to be done, it is safer, of course, to buy as large a part of the equipment as possible, new. In other lines of the Manual Arts work, very little disposition is shown to buy second hand machinery and tools; but there seems to be a decided tendency to look for old equipment for the printshop. This, perhaps, arises out of the misapprehension that even a very small printing plant is very expensive. On the contrary, it will be seen by reference to the lists on page 58, that a printing equipment is comparatively inexpensive. Unless one is an expert, or is familiar with the time and kind of use the goods have been subjected to, it is unsafe to buy such used goods as type, leads, slugs, rule, furniture, and type cases, for these may be regarded as perishable; besides, they are comparatively cheap. So, from the financial standpoint, as well as that of good work, it is unwise to buy such used material. And when it comes to the larger, more expensive articles, like the press and the cutter, it must be considered that they are probably not soon, if ever, to be replaced, that imperfections are difficult to detect, and that not a very large reduction, can be had on machines in good repair. But if it is a question of getting a start in printing by the use of old equipment or doing without the printshop, by all means let's have the old equipment. There are a good many items that can be safely and cheaply bought second hand. Among these are cabinets, stones and frames, case stands, lead cases, etc.

It is wise to buy only such staple articles as in a good printer's judgment the conditions demand. There is some temptation to buy, out of a scanty allowance, articles which are not absolutely necessary, or which may easily be improvised. It is wise to buy the essentials and such quantities and accessories as make what one buys available to its full capacity. To illustrate, it is not uncommon to find quite a liberal quantity of type with an insufficient supply of quads and spaces. This simply means that the type is available for use only to the extent of the quad and space supply. This illustration is only typical of a number that might be made. For school purpose, it is much more satisfactory to have generous quantities of a few sizes of type of one series, than to have small quantities of several sizes and series. If the specific purposes of the shop are clearly in mind, the selection of faces, quantities, and sizes of type is greatly facilitated.

If it is planned to do very much of the supplementary reading work for the elementary grades, good quantities of 12 point type should be provided, including such a special supply of sorts, especially in capitals, as seems necessary to meet the needs. For instance, it has been found that in the language and reading work of the lower grades, the personal pronouns, I and we, are used with great extravagance in beginning sentences; so the I and W boxes are soon empty. In case some prominence is to be given to arithmetic work, then larger quantities of figures, fractions, etc., should be bought than come in the regular fonts. For general work, there can be no wiser selection than a large quantity of 10 point type. Of course, where the allowance permits, it is extremely nice to have small fonts of two or three different faces, which may be used for variety, initials, display, etc.

It has been found very satisfactory to have large quantities of a few sizes of body type as previously suggested, and in addition, a few fonts of a heavier face, duplicating the body type in sizes but with some larger sizes, and also a small assortment of some nice simple text letters. In selecting type, a wide, clear, readable face is desirable, and it is best to select those faces which do not contain hair lines or complications which make it difficult to get a distinct impression, and which render the type less durable. It is rather unusual to see a shop sufficiently supplied with quads and spaces, and especially is this so where much of the work is widely spaced and where each line is treated as a paragraph, as in elementary matter.

In order to provide for the small font display type which, of course, comes in straight letter work, it has been found a good plan to add, in addition to the regular 20%, 5 pounds each of quads and spaces for each 50 pounds, and 2½ pounds for each 25 pounds of body type.

Everything considered, the 10 × 15 press is preferable for the school as well as other work. It accommodates large forms, which fact is often urged against it; but for the smaller work, like the most of the school work, it is practically as easily handled as an 8 × 12. It is considerably more expensive but it has a much greater capacity for work of the more advanced kind.

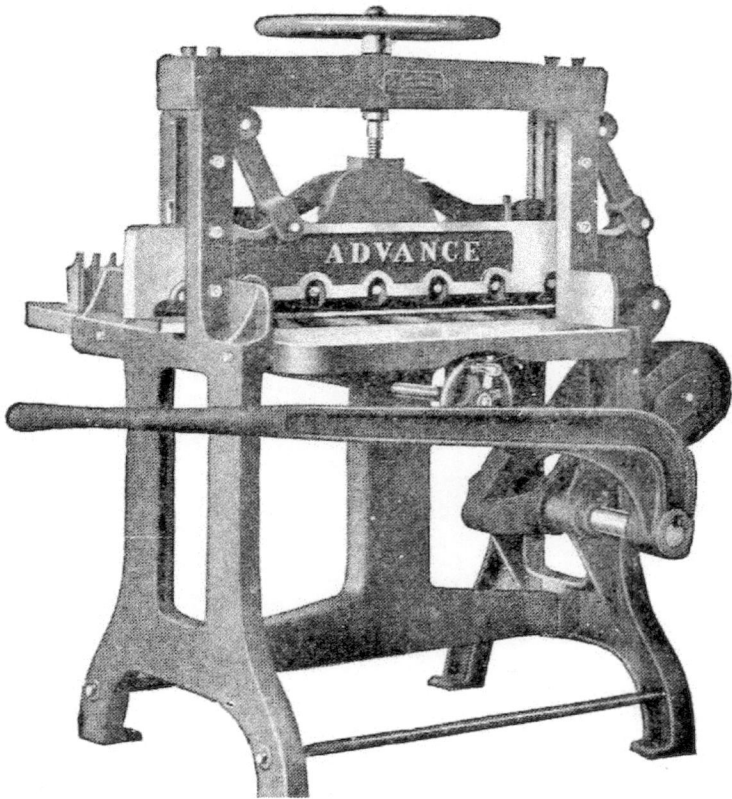

Fig. 30.

Of course, cabinets are preferable to open case stands. They are compact, free from dust and dirt, and of good appearance. However, they are more expensive than stands, if the matter must be determined by the question of cost. If one goes to the expense of getting a cutter, Fig. 30, it is the part of good judgment to get one that will be of the greatest service. So it is advisable to get a 25 or 26 inch cutter. The difference in cost above that of a twenty-two inch is overbalanced by the economy and convenience in cutting large stock. In case a large cutter cannot be bought, small table cutters, which give good service, may be had at various low prices. The stone mentioned in the $800 list on this page is practically ideal for the small printshop. It is a 26 × 44 marble, mounted upon a cabinet which contains a large quantity of wood furniture, and a number of drawers and letter boards. This stone is not so much more expensive after all, if one considers the cost of the furniture and case and the other conveniences.

Probably the general method of selecting equipment for any line of work is to take an ideal list and by elimination reduce it to within the limits of the appropriation. The following $800 equipment is the one selected by the author for his own classes, after several years of planning and investigation. During this time, a great many school men who have had to deal with the same problem, and a number of expert printers were consulted and asked for criticism of the proposed list under the conditions which the equipment has to meet:

1   ½ h. p. motor.

1   10 × 15 Chandler & Price Gordon Press with 3 chases.

1   Steel chase.

1   Boston Staple Binder, Style A.

1   26" Chandler & Price Paper Cutter.

1   Utility Imposing Stone Frame and Stone, 26 × 44.

1   No. 68 New Departure Cabinet (50 cases).

1   No. 2 Paper and Card Stock Cabinet.

1	No. 8 Bettis Lead and Slug Case.
2	Pairs news cases.
2	Pair 2–3 case tilting brackets.
1	Metal furniture case.
1	No. 1 Harris Rule Case.
5	$8\frac{3}{4} \times 13$ all brass galleys.
1	12×18 all brass galley.
8	$8 \times 2\frac{1}{4}$ Yankee Job Sticks.
1	$18 \times 2\frac{1}{2}$ Yankee Job Stick.
2	Doz. No. 1 Wickersham Quoins.

2	Keys, No. 1.
1	Doz. Spring Tongue Gauge Pins.
1	Quart Success benzine can.
1	Benzine brush.
1	No. 2 press brake.
1	3 × 6 planer.
1	3½ × 8 proof planer.
1	2½ × 4½ mallet.
2	Pair roller supporters.
20	Pounds 6 Point Authors Roman Wide.

40	Pounds 8 Point Authors Roman Wide.
40	Pounds 10 Point Authors Roman Wide.
20	Pounds 12 Point Authors Roman Wide.
20	Pounds 18 Point Authors Roman Wide.
2	Fonts 6 Point Old Roman Black.
2	Fonts 8 Point Old Roman Black.
2	Fonts 10 Point Old Roman Black.
2	Fonts 12 Point Old Roman Black.
2	Fonts 18 Point Old Roman Black.
1	Font 24 Point Old Roman Black.

1	Font 30 Point Old Roman Black.
1	Font 36 Point Old Roman Black.
1	Font 48 Point Old Roman Black.
1	Font 8 Point Engraver's Old Black.
4	Fonts 12 Point Engraver's Old Black, L. C.
2	Fonts 12 Point Engraver's Old Black, Caps.
1	Font 24 Point Engraver's Old Black.
1	Font 48 Point Elzeverine Initials.
5	Pounds 6 point spaces assorted.
10	Pounds 8 point spaces assorted.

10	Pounds 10 point spaces assorted.
10	Pounds 12 point spaces assorted.
10	Pounds 18 point spaces assorted.
5	Pounds 24 point spaces assorted.
5	Pounds 30 point spaces assorted.
5	Pounds 36 point spaces assorted.
5	Pounds 48 point spaces assorted.
5	Pounds 6 point quads assorted.
10	Pounds 8 point quads assorted.
10	Pounds 10 point quads assorted.

10	Pounds 10 point 2- and 3-em quads.
5	Pounds each 12, 18, 24 point quads assorted.
5	Pounds each 30, 36, 48 point quads assorted.
10	Pounds 10 point leaders, three dots to em.
10	Pounds 8 point leaders, three dots to em.
50	Pounds each 2 point L. S. leads and 6 point L. S. slugs.
3	Pounds L. S. brass rule hair line, side centered on 2 point body.
3	Pounds L. S. brass rule, 1 point face, side centered on 2 point body.
2	Pounds 2 point L. S. black face rule.
2	Pounds 4 point L. S. black face rule.

2	Pounds 6 point L. S. black face rule.
2	Pounds 10 point L. S. black face rule.
24	Pounds metal furniture.
1	Font No. 1 brass and copper spaces.
4	Font solid brass panel ends.
1	Set 12 point brass squares.
100	1×3 brass label holders.
5M	¼" Boston staples.

In case this amount of money is not available for a printing equipment, this list may be modified to come within the necessary limit. By substituting a smaller press and cutter, by getting stands instead of cabinets for the type and stone, by eliminating the stock cabinet, motor, and stapler, and by reducing the quantities of various items, one may still have an excellent equipment. The following is such a suggestive list, and can be bought for $400:

Press, 8" × 12" with four chases.

Cutter, 23½".

½   Doz. job sticks.

1   Doz. gauge pins.

1   Doz. quoins.

2   Keys.

1   Benzine can.

1   Benzine brush.

1   Waste can.

½   Doz. brass galleys, 8¾" × 13".

10	Lbs. metal furniture.
1	Two lb. font labor saving brass rule, 1 point, side centered on 2 point body.
1	Two lb. font brass rule, labor saving, 2 point.
50	Lbs. L. S. leads, 2 point.
25	Lbs. L. S. slugs, 6 point.
1	Rule case.
1	Metal furniture case.
1	Planer.
1	Proof planer.
1	Mallet.

1	Lead and slug case.
1	Case wood furniture.
24	California job cases.
2	Pairs news cases.
1	Double case stand, 24 cases.
1	Stone and frame, 26" × 44".
10	Pounds 8 point type.
50	Pounds 10 point type.
25	Pounds 12 point type.
2	Fonts 18 point type.

1	Font 24 point type.
5	Pounds 8 point quads and spaces.
15	Pounds 10 point quads and spaces.
10	Pounds 12 point quads and spaces.
5	Pounds 18 point quads and spaces.
2½	Pounds 24 point quads and spaces.

Fig. 31.

ARRANGEMENT AND DISPOSITION OF EQUIPMENT

If the machinery, cabinets, tables, etc., are compactly and properly arranged in good relative positions, a good job outfit can be placed and used in much smaller quarters than at first seems possible. The printshop is one place where a great amount of floor space between the various parts of the equipment is not entirely essential. When the groups or individuals have been set to work, there is no necessity for a great amount of passing back and forth. This is mentioned for the benefit of those who feel that printing cannot be installed unless there is an enormous amount of floor space available. Of course, large rooms are desirable, but after all, the effectiveness and availability of the equipment turn on the point of convenient arrangement of related parts, so that a job may pass easily from one stage to another without disturbance or interruption. In other words, the arrangement must be such that all the operations of the job shop may be in progress at the same time and that without confusion. In the first place, the type cabinet or case stand should be convenient to plenty of table space so that the boys may carry their cases back and forth without difficulty.

The proof stand or press and the imposing stone should be of easy access to those who are working at the type case and at the same time in close reach of the pressman.

A good position for the press is in a well lighted corner far enough from the walls to permit easy passing of the pressman for the purpose of oiling, cleaning, and general care of the press. The motor may be placed in the corner back of the press and entirely out of the way. The paper cutter and stock cabinet should be placed as closely together as possible not to interfere with the action of each other. There cannot well be too much in the way of drawers, wall cases, and shelving, for the work of the students, small items of supplies, inks, rollers, benzine and waste cans, etc. These conveniences can be added here and there in small, unoccupied spaces, with just a little time and a very small bit of expense. In this way and this only, can a place be provided for everything with any assurance that everything, at any one time, may be found in its place. These repositories should be properly labelled. Such additional items and conveniences not included in any list of equipment, are nevertheless among the essentials, and their presence greatly facilitates and systematizes the work. The matter of table space cannot be too greatly emphasized. Not only are tables used for rests for type cases but the make-up galleys are laid upon them for convenience in work. Proof reading also requires table space.

It seems proper, under this heading to speak of the disposition of the various sizes of type for the greatest convenience. Of course, the type ought to be divided and placed so as to be accessible to the greatest possible number. So, except in very small fonts, each size should be divided and put into as many cases as can be supplied with working quantities of type. Thus, fifty pounds of ten point, which is extensively used in general work, may be divided among five or even more cases. In this way, ten pupils can be accommodated at the ten point cases at one time, since two can work, to a very fair advantage, at one case.

The class works in groups, one setting type, one proofing and correcting, one making up forms, while the fourth operates the press. At the same time, there usually are jobs going forward in different kinds and sizes of type. So, it is difficult to think of needing accommodations for more than ten students at one size and kind of type at one time.

The little boy said, "I can not go home.

My goat ran into the woods.

He will not go home."

Then the boy began to cry.

The squirrel tried to make the goat go home.

Do you best your very best,
And do it every day;
Little boys and little girls,
This is the wisest way.

See-saw! See-saw!
Here we go up and down.
See-saw! See-saw!
This is the way to town.

The world's a very happy
    place, where every child
    should dance and sing,
And always have a smiling
    face,
And never sulk for anything.

    Politeness is to do or say

HIGH SCHOOL
COMMERCIAL DEPARTMENT

Bloomington, Illinois.

It was late in mild October, and the long autumnal rain
Had left the summer harvest-fields all green with grass again:
The first sharp frosts had fallen, leaving all the woodlands gay
With the hues of summer's rainbow, or the meadow-flowers of May.

—Whittier.

PRINT SHOP PRESS

Ye Highe Schoole.

Vol. I.　　　SIOUX CITY, IOWA, THURSDAY, NOVEMBER 27, 1913.　　　No. 1.

ORGANIZED PLAY

THIS IDEA IS BEING CARRIED OUT
IN SIOUX CITY.

in Sioux City. He visits each school
about once a week. He starts the pupils
in some kind of play and the teacher
continues this until Mr. Morris returns
the next week. All pupils are engaged

Henry Mentzerr

FLYING THE FLAG

H. H. RICE COMMENTS ON THE
SUBJECT.

Reynolds Low

Hawthorne Mother's Club
Meets Tuesday
September 23, 1913
3:15 o'clock

HISTORY

Senior Eighth Grade, December 1, 1913
9:30 to 11:30 A. M.

NOTE: Answer any ten of the following twelve questions.

I. For what are the following places to be remembered?

a.   Jamestown.   *c.*   Harper's Ferry.

b.   Vicksburg.   *d.*   Yorktown.

HISTORY

Senior Eighth Grade, December 1, 1913
9:30 to 11:30 A. M.

NOTE: Answer any ten of the following twelve questions.

I. For what are the following places to be remembered?

      a. Jamestown.   *c.* Harper's Ferry.
      b. Vicksburg.   *d.* Yorktown.

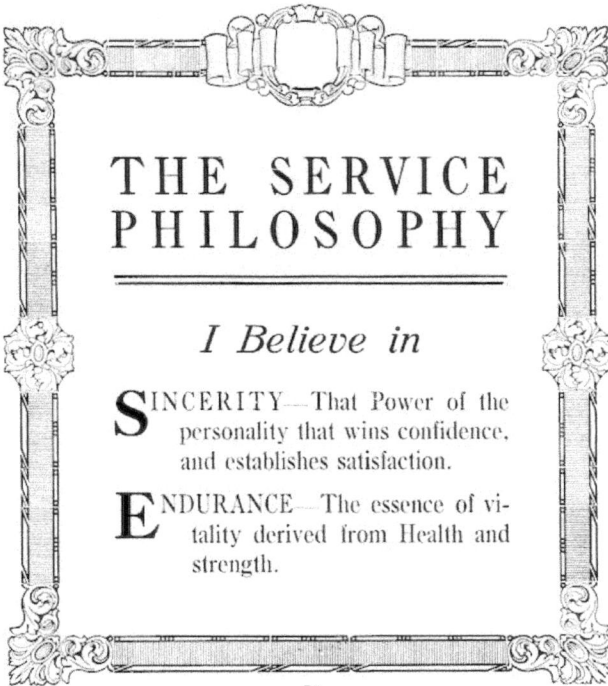

THE SERVICE PHILOSOPHY

I Believe in

SINCERITY—That Power of the personality that wins confidence, and establishes satisfaction.

ENDURANCE—The essence of vitality derived from Health and strength.

INTRODUCTION

There are a number of well defined reasons why bookbinding may justly claim recognition as an educational factor in our schools.

In the first place, the permanent and vital character of the book in one form or another has given it a place of respect in all civilizations. The book is the final form of all enduring literature and indeed of all enduring thought. It is the epitome of the printer's, the engraver's, the illustrator's, the designer's, and the binder's art, and is the meeting point of all the crafts.

So the book idea appeals very strongly to people both in and out of school. Bookbinding is perhaps the most logical and consistent of all the crafts, in its development from the simple to the more complex forms. In this easy gradation, is repeated the history of the book itself and of its development.

From this point of view, books fall into four rather distinct classes.

1. The simplest idea of binding is the holding together in some manner, a number of single leaves. So the attention is directed simply to methods of fastening together leaves of related matter for convenience in handling.

2. After this simple convenience has been met, the matter of protecting the leaves forces itself upon us, and the attention is turned almost wholly to devising ways of making durable and beautiful covers. The various forms of separate covers are made to accomplish these ends.

3. Later, the attention turns back to the book proper and the different methods of putting together a number of sections which become necessary in larger books made of folded printed sheets. The emphasis now naturally falls upon this new feature of fastening sections together, and so, various methods of sewing are developed.

4. In the fourth division, the emphasis goes upon the covers and the decoration. Here come in the tooling, lettering, inlaying and such processes as are usually included in the term finishing.

APPLY TO CHILDREN'S WORK.

Not only is the book idea enduring and vital, and its development logical and consistent, but the book work may be intimately related to the other activities of the school, the pupil bringing about with his own effort the satisfaction of his own distinct needs.

In making books for spelling, reading, language, nature study, art, etc., these needs and relations are evident.

These books with their stories, their covers, and their end papers, offer abundant material for illustration, design, lettering, etc., in the art work.

Again, the bookbinding work in its elementary aspects of construction is peculiarly adapted to children. This is evidenced by the fact, easily demonstrated, that children do as well in their particular grades of work as matured but inexperienced people can do in the same grades of work.

Aside from the logical development and the genuineness of the problems presented and their intimate relations to the other work, perhaps the strongest argument in favor of bookbinding in the schools, is the fact of its adaptability to the conditions of the ordinary school room, with but little equipment and hence but little expense.

The work may be carried on in the primary and intermediate grades with as small, but practically the same equipment, as is necessary for such activities as "cardboard construction" and kindred work.

It will be seen by reference to page 45 how inexpensive even a good equipment for upper grade and high school work is.

CLASSES OF BINDINGS.

Forwarding—Finishing.

In advanced bookbinding, there are the two general divisions of work:—Forwarding, which includes in new books, sewing, backing, putting on boards, and covering; and finishing, which has to do with the lettering, tooling, inlaying, and general decorative treatment.

The elementary and high school treatment of the subject of bookbinding, such a treatment as is undertaken in the present volume, is almost wholly concerned with the various processes included in the term Forwarding, which in rebinding includes a number of other steps not mentioned above.

Case Binding; Library Binding; Extra Binding.

Based upon their methods of sewing, backing, covering, finishing, etc., there may be said to be three general classes of bindings:—Case Binding, Library Binding, and Extra Binding. These are arbitrary terms applied to methods of binding which have been fully established and recognized.

In the modern commercial binderies, all kinds of modifications, combinations and imitations are made, so that it is often difficult to tell by external appearances of bindings to what types they belong.

It is a common thing to see a case binding in full leather.

The proper way to have a book bound or rebound is to have written specifications which indicate details of methods, materials, etc.

The following are typical specifications for Case Binding:—

1. Plates guarded.

2. Sewed all along with five punctures and kettlestitches.

3. Full or half buckram.

4. Glued and backed.

5. Attached back.

6. Commercial silk headband.

7. First and last leaves used as pastedowns.

8. Edges uncut.

II.
CASE BINDING.

Case Bindings or casings (for the craft binder refuses to call them bindings) are those covers which are made separately from the books and laid on. These covers have the characteristics enumerated in the specifications and are the unsubstantial covers usually found on modern cheap, temporary books.

If the book is to be bound from original sheets, each sheet is folded into a section. Such a section is called a signature. The number of leaves in a folded sheet or section gives the name to the book. A sheet folded once, making two leaves, is a folio; twice, making four leaves, a quarto or 4to; three times, making eight leaves, an octavo or 8vo; four times, making sixteen leaves, a 16mo; etc. It is seen by this that owing to the varying sizes of paper, any form of book may vary greatly in size. However, the following may be taken as a general standard of sizes:—

16mo 5×7 inches.

Octavo (8vo) 6×9 inches.

Quarto (4to) 10×12½ inches.

End Paper

If there have not been left an abundance of blank leaves at the first and last of the book, at least four folios are cut—two for each end—and these become the first and last sections of the book.

The sections are now assembled in proper order, a tin is placed between sections at several places in the book and all are put under heavy pressure. This is usually done at the last of a recitation, and the book left in press over night, so that the sections may be perfectly flat.

Mark Up—Puncture.

After the book is carefully evened up by knocking the back and head against the table, it is marked up; that is, a mark is put on each outside endpaper near the head, so that the head of the book may be recognized without opening; and then places are marked for five punctures along the back. The top puncture may be put about three-fourths of an inch or an inch from the head, and the bottom one about one and one-fourth or one and one-half inches from the foot. It is considered that the head should be somewhat stronger, since it must bear the strain of pulling the book from the shelf.

Then with a small saw or a sharp-edged file, punctures are made across the back at the marks. These should be just deep enough to reach through the inside folio of each section.

Sewing First Two Sections.

Now the book is ready to sew. It is placed on the table to the left of the workman with the back toward him and the head to the left. With a linen thread and a long, slim needle ready, the workman takes up the section of endpapers lying on top and turns it entirely over, laying it exactly in front of him with the head to his right. Fig. 14. With his right hand he inserts the needle into the head puncture, while with his left hand in the middle of the section between the leaves, he draws the needle through to the inside and runs it out at the foot puncture. "In at the head puncture and out at the foot." The second section is turned over upon the first, and the needle run in at the foot puncture and out at the second puncture from the foot. Then it is inserted at the second puncture from the foot of the first section and immediately run out at the same puncture but on the opposite side of the thread which runs along inside the first section. Then apply this unfailing rule when in doubt as to what puncture to go into:—"Put the needle into a puncture so located that it will not undo work already done, and that the thread will not be left exposed on the outside of the book."

Applying this rule, it is seen that the needle must be put into the second puncture of the second section. This operation is repeated at each puncture until the head is reached. When the needle has been drawn from the head puncture of the second section, the threads coming out of the two head punctures are pulled up tight and are tied into a double knot. a Fig. 14. Care must be used in pulling the thread so as not to tear the paper.

Kettlestitch;—Sewing All along.

The third section is now laid on and the needle run in at the head puncture and out at the second puncture from the head. Now comes the elusive "kettlestitch." The needle is run *under* the second section at the right of the second puncture and out at the left of the same puncture, as at b Fig. 14. The thread is drawn loosely so as to leave a small loop through which the needle is passed. It is now drawn taut and the needle run back into the second puncture of the third section. This stitch is made every time the needle comes *out* of a puncture until the sewing is finished. When the last puncture is reached, a double kettlestitch is made and the thread cut a half inch from the knot. This is what is meant by "sewing all along." If the original thread should not be long enough or should break, a new thread is tied on with a weaver's knot, Fig. 15, always inside the book and as closely as possible to the puncture to avoid pulling the knot through the next puncture.

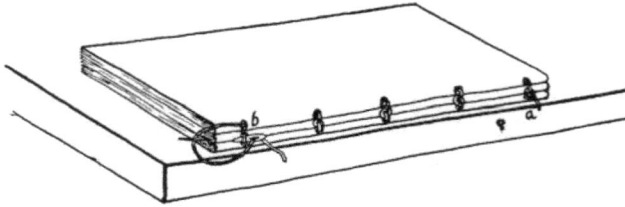

Fig. 14. Sewing all along.
a. first two sections tied.
b. Kettlestitch.

Fig. 15.

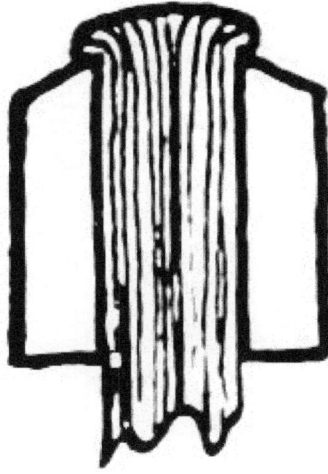

Fig. 16.

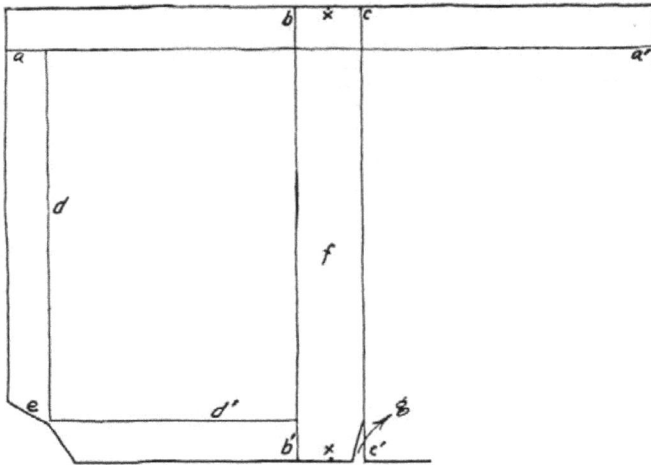

Fig. 17. Marking of cloth for Case Binding.

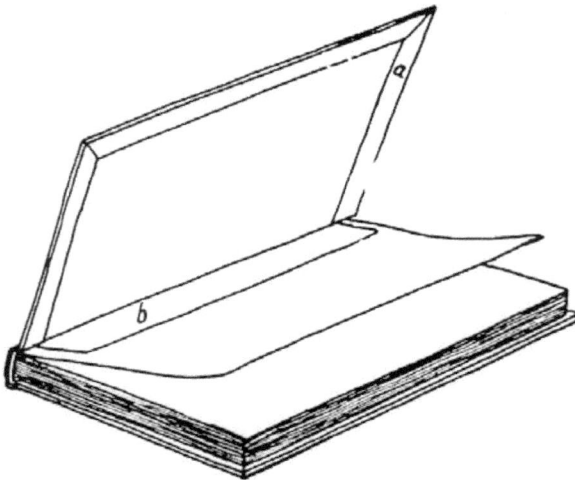

Fig. 18. Laying on of the cover.

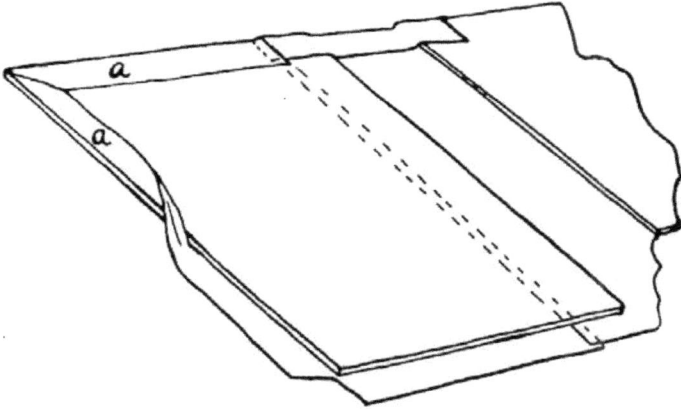

Fig. 19. Half cloth cover showing turn-ins at a.

Backing boards—Backing.

The book is now placed between backing boards with only a small portion of the book projecting above the boards and then put into the lying press (1. Plate 1), and clamped up tightly. The part projecting should about equal the thickness of the cardboard used for the cover.

This book is not to be rounded any more than is absolutely necessary in the backing. The process of backing is necessary because of a thickened condition of the back as a result of the numerous threads and perhaps a few guards that have been added to it. By clamping the book tightly and hammering the back, the thickness can be reduced by forcing the edges over the boards as at Fig. 16.

After the book is firmly fastened in the press, the back is covered with thin glue, which is rubbed in with a stiff brush and then wiped off, so that it remains only in the little depressions between the sections. Within about fifteen minutes, the glue reaches a kind of elastic condition, and then the hammer is brought into use.

By light strokes along the center of the back, and then gradually farther out toward the end sections, the edges of the sections are forced away from the center and made to project finally over the edges of the backing boards, making the joint.

PLATE I

1. Lying Press
2. Backing Boards
3. Bone Folder
4. Paper Cutter
5. Head Knife
6. Sewing Frame
7. Backing Sticks
8. Letter Press used as Standing Press
9. Back Saw
10. Joint Rods
11. Pressing Tin
12. Pressing Board

Super;—Headband;—Back Strip.

When the book is dry, a piece of super or thin canvas is glued to the back and about one and one-half inches down the endpapers, which are then cut off along the edges of this super. This forms what is called the slip. The super should be a little shorter than the book and about two or three inches wider than the back of the book.

A piece of cotton or silk stock headband is now glued to the back at the head and projecting about one-eighth of an inch above it. Then a strip of thick, tough paper, just large enough to cover the back, is glued on. This finishes the book ready for the cover.

Squares;—Foredge.

During the processes just described, while waiting for the glue to dry, the materials are gotten for the cover. Two boards are cut as wide as the book and from one-fourth to three-eighths of an inch longer. This makes the squares one-eighth or three-sixteenths of an inch and determines the width of the joint at the back, since the board must go forward sufficiently to make the projection at the foredge the same as at the head and foot. This projection is called the squares.

Several things must be considered in determining the size of the squares. The most important are protection, strength, and beauty. From the standpoint of good proportion, of course, the large, thick book would demand large squares, whereas protection of the edges may not require them so long; while the strength and durability of the binding would suggest shorter squares still.

A large book set upon a shelf is forced by its own weight down between the boards against the shelf, straining or breaking the cover at the back.

Turn-in;—Size of Cover Cloth.

In cutting leather, cloth, and paper, it is a rule to allow three-fourths of an inch for each turn-in. So this is observed in cutting material for this cover. To find the size of the cloth for a full cloth cover, it is necessary to add together the widths of the two boards, the thickness of the back, the two joints and one and one-half inches for the turn-ins at the foredge. This sum gives the dimension, of course, from the foredge of one cover around the back to the foredge of the other cover. The dimension of the cloth lengthwise of the book is one and one-half inches greater than the length of the board.

To make the cover, the cloth is laid wrong side up on the table, Fig. 17. Three-fourths of an inch is measured down from the top and a pencil line is drawn, a, a'. Then the middle of the cloth from left to right is found and marked as indicated by the crosses. From these central points, the lines b b' and c c' are located which mark the positions of the back edges of the boards and of course, are as far apart as the thickness of the book plus the two joints. Then the boards are placed so that they fit into the right angles formed by lines bb' and cc' and aa', and a pencil mark as dd' is made along the foredge and bottom of each board, completing the rectangles. The strips of cloth outside these rectangles are the turn-ins.

Mitres.

With scissors or a knife the corners are clipped out as at e, which is called making the mitres. It is clear that if the corner were cut entirely up to the corner of the rectangle, there would be danger of exposing the corner of the board, so a distance is left about equal to the thickness of the board.

Pasting.

The surface of the cloth except the back strip between the boards, is covered with a thin coat of paste, the boards are laid on, and the edges of the cloth are turned over the edges of the boards and pressed down as at a, Figs. 18 and 19, care being taken to get the cloth firmly against the edges of the boards.

With less mature pupils, it is sometimes advisable to put on only one board at a time, in which case the head and foot of the back strip are treated as at g, Fig. 17. The cover is now ready for the press. It is closed in book fashion with a pressing tin or board between the covers. A piece of clean waste paper is put between each board and the pressing tin or board. A waste paper and a board are placed on each side of the cover and all put into the press. The cover should be left in the press over night. The waste paper is very important. Without it, the tins are likely to stick to the book and the moisture of the paste to cause rust which mars the book. This caution is never out of place and can never be repeated too often, i. e., do not use too thin paste; do not use too much paste; put on the paste rapidly.

Laid On.

Now the cover is ready to be laid on. A strip of tough paper just as wide and as long as the back of the book, is now pasted along the back cloth between the boards f, Fig. 17, and inserted under the cloth which is turned over at the two ends.

If the cover were to be left hollow, the paste would be applied to the slips only; but in this case, where the back cloth is to be attached, both the slips and the back, as well as the strip between the boards of the cover, are thoroughly covered with paste, and the book set into the cover in its proper position. While the workman supports the book with one hand, he brings up one side of the cover firmly against the book. The slip on this side becomes attached to the board. Then the book is laid down on the side just pasted, while the other cover is pulled firmly to bring the back cloth against the book, and is then pressed down upon the paste-covered slip or super b, Fig. 18. Examination is then made to see if the book is straight in the cover, if the squares are correct, etc. If it is not straight, it is removed and the process repeated.

When the cover is on straight, the cloth is rubbed firmly along the back and into the joints. When it is thoroughly attached at the back, the book is put lightly into the press, after a tin, inserted between two papers, has been put between the cover and the book on each side.

Paste-downs—Bone Folder.

The next step is the pasting down of the endpapers. The cover is lifted on one side and a piece of waste paper is placed beneath the endpaper which is then covered with paste.

This done, the endpaper is drawn back upon the board and rubbed down with the hands. Then with a bone folder, 3, Plate I, the endpaper and slip are rubbed under the back edge of the board at the joint.

The cover is now closed upon the book and immediately opened. If it is found that in closing, the endpaper wrinkles or proves in anyway wrong, the wrinkles are smoothed out and other defects corrected. If necessary, the endpaper may be lifted carefully from the board and then put down again. Then the cover is closed again, and again inspected. If it is all right, the other endpaper is treated in like manner, and the book is put lightly into press, not neglecting waste paper and tins, and left until thoroughly dry.

Paste.

The best paste is made as follows:—Add one-half a teaspoonsful of powdered alum and a few drops of wintergreen to one pint of flour. Mix with water to the consistency of cream. Cook until it becomes stiff and waxlike, stirring constantly. Then pour in some hot water, stir and cook again until it becomes the desired consistency. Ordinary library paste or photo mount is not satisfactory.

III.
LIBRARY BINDING.

The name Library Binding may be somewhat misleading if one has in mind the bindings commonly seen in libraries. This binding is practically what was recommended for the libraries of England by a committee from the English Society of Arts, appointed to investigate the causes of the lack of durability in bindings and to suggest remedies for defects found.

The following specifications indicate the distinguishing features of this binding:—

1.

Half leather, paper sides.

2.

Sewed on four or more tapes.

3.

Double boards.

4.

French joint.

5.

Zigzag colored endpapers.

6.

Head cut, out of boards, and colored.

7.

Backed and slightly rounded.

8.

Cord inserted under leather instead of headband.

9.

Leather attached to back.

Zigzag Endpaper.

After the sheets are folded and pressed as described in the previous binding, the zigzag endpapers are prepared. In cutting these endpapers, four sheets of white paper to match the book are cut and folded, two of the folios being considerably wider than the book so as to allow for the fold e, Fig. 20. Each leaf of the large folios is folded back about one-fourth of an inch from the original fold. Then another folio, c, the same size as the book, is pasted under zigzag e, and the endpapers made in this way become the first and last sections. Folio b is the colored endpaper which is not inserted until book is sewed.

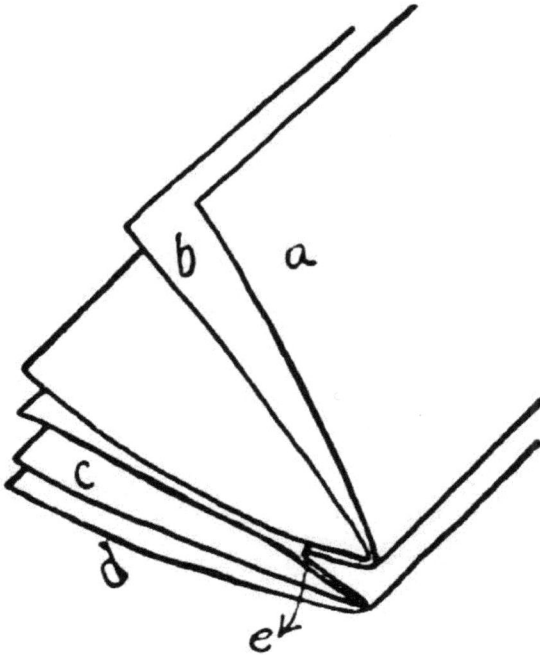

Fig. 20. Zigzag end. a, b, c, separate folios.

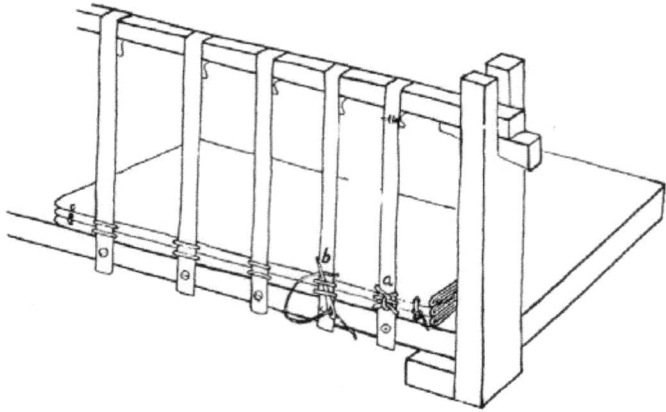

Fig. 21. Sewing Frame and sewing on tapes. a, finished catch or crowsfoot stitch. b, the beginning of the catchstitch.

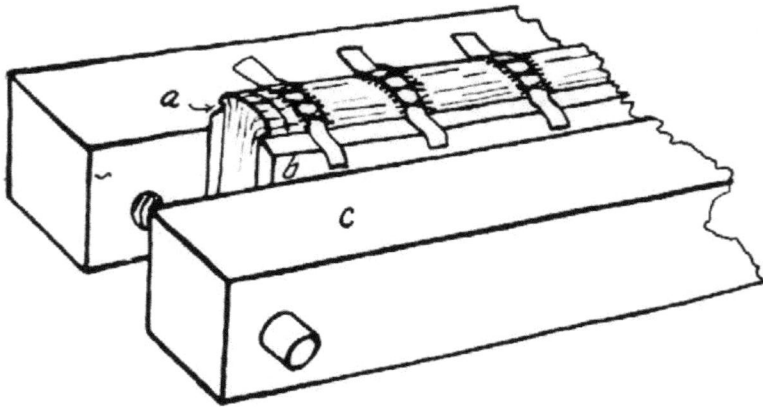

Fig. 22. Ready for backing. a, Joint. b, Backing boards. c, Lying, or finishing press.

Fig. 23. putting on double boards. a, The slip.

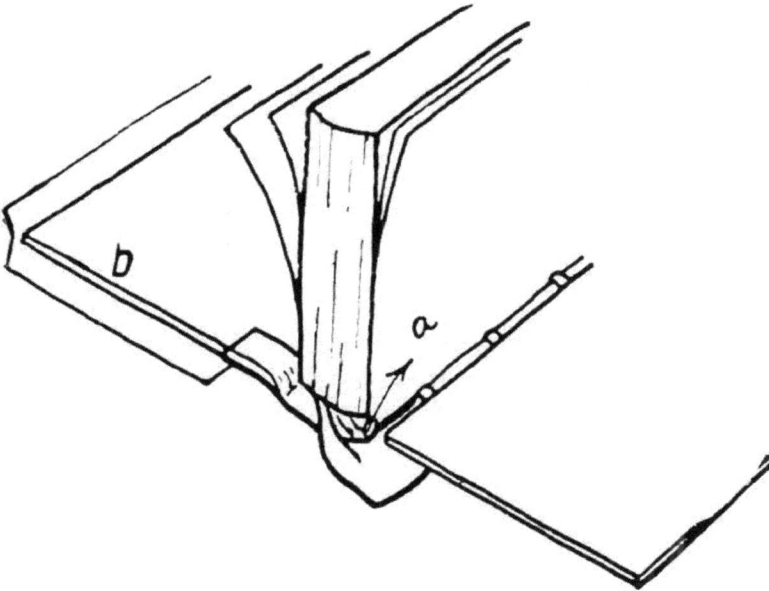

Fig. 24. Putting on the leather back. a, cord.

The book is now marked up as in the Case Binding except that there are only two punctures, one about three-quarters of an inch from the head, and the other about one and one-quarter inches from the foot, in an ordinary size of book.

Sewing on Tapes.

Sewing on tapes requires a sewing frame, Fig. 21, which is prepared for sewing by tying five tapes to the horizontal bar. The book is then laid on the floor of the frame with the head toward the right and the back to the tapes. The head tape is placed one-fourth of an inch to the left of the head puncture, while the foot tape is placed one-fourth of an inch to the right of the foot puncture. The other tapes are distributed equally along the distance between those at the head and foot. All the tapes are fastened to the edge of the frame floor with thumb tacks. Of course, that is only one simple frame out of a great variety which may be made. There are numerous ways of improvising sewing frames. Temporary frames are often made by tacking small strips to the ends of drawing boards, and fastening a cross bar to them. In large classes, merely a board is sometimes used as in olden times, when stiff thongs or strips of vellum were used. This is not very satisfactory.

The book is laid to the left as in the previous binding, and the sections are turned in the same way, and laid upon the frame. The end section is laid with a, Fig. 20, on the floor of the frame and the needle inserted at the head puncture of the fold between e and d through folio c, Fig. 20. Then with the left hand, the needle is drawn in and run back out just to the right of the head tape. Then the needle is run into the section immediately to the left of the head tape, making a stitch across the tape. This is repeated at each tape and finally the needle comes out at the foot puncture. Now the second section is put on, the needle inserted at the foot puncture and the sewing continued as in the first section, until the head puncture is reached, when the thread is tied with a double knot to the original end. The third section is now put on and treated exactly like the first section until the needle comes out at the right of the head tape, when a crow's foot or catch stitch is made in the following way:—

Crow's Foot or Catch Stitch.

As the needle comes out at the side of the tape, instead of sewing the thread straight across the tape as before, the needle is run from the bottom up behind the two previous threads in such a way as to make a loop knot around them, a and b, Fig 21. Then the needle is run into the section on the opposite side of the tape exactly as in previous stitches. This is repeated at every tape until the foot puncture is reached, where a kettlestitch is made. After the third section, a kettlestitch is made every time the needle comes out at an end puncture, and a crow's foot or catch stitch every third or fourth section.

The remainder of the book is sewed by exact repetitions of the processes thus far described.

When the sewing is completed, the tapes are cut, leaving them about one and one-half inches long at each side and a colored folio, b, Fig. 20, is tipped to the top of each zigzag as at e, and the book is then ready for gluing, rounding and backing.

Rounding.

Rounding, as the name implies, is the process of giving a convex shape to the back of a book to prevent its becoming sunken or concave. The book is laid upon the table, and the first few sections are pulled firmly forward, while with a hammer, the upper edge of the back is struck lightly, driving the upper sections forward. Then the book is turned over and the process is repeated on the other side.

A folded sheet of waste paper is tipped (pasted by a very narrow strip of paste) along the sides of the book at the back.

Marks are placed about one-eighth of an inch from the back, showing the places for the edges of the backing boards between which the book is put and all clamped into the lying press, Fig. 22. This done, the back is thoroughly covered with thin glue which is rubbed in with a stiff brush and wiped as in the previous book. Within fifteen or twenty minutes, when the glue has dried sufficiently to be rubbery, the back is pounded with a hammer, striking first along the center, then gradually toward the end sections, always with a gliding blow, until the edges have been forced over the tops of the backing boards, as a, Fig. 22. If this has been properly done, the back will be smooth and rounding, and the edges will project over about the thickness of the boards.

The tapes are now pasted down against the outside leaves of the endpapers, and the super glued on, reaching from puncture to puncture, and to the ends of the tapes on each side. When dry, the endpapers, to which the tapes were pasted, are cut off around the edges of the super, a, Fig. 23. Material is now gotten ready for the cover. Since this book is to have a French joint, the boards are cut as much narrower than the book as will make the proper width of joint; and since it is to have double boards, four boards are cut, two thin and two medium. A thin board and a thicker one are glued together, all except about two inches along the back edge, to form one board. The boards, thus glued, are put into the press, and the leather cut, which is to be one and one-half inches longer than the board and wide enough to reach around the back and as far down the sides as desired—the general rule being "more than a fourth and less than a third." This, however, is a statement of the most general kind, and proper widths for the leather are determined to meet specific conditions.

Skiving—Head Cut—Coloring.

With a sharp skiving or head knife, 5, Plate I, the edges of the leather are pared thin, and also a strip through the middle where the back of the book goes, is pared, if the leather is quite thick. For this operation, the leather should be laid on a stone or slate.

The book is now marked with pencil and trysquare where the head is to be cut, and is placed between two pressing boards with a heavy piece of cardboard, called the cut-against, between the back pressing board and the book. In this condition, the book is now put into the cutting press, Plate II, the front pressing board being pushed down on a level with the mark on the book and with the top of the press. The plow is run forward and backward, the blade meanwhile being gradually screwed toward the book, cutting only a very few leaves at a stroke. With this easy stroke and slow advance of the blade, if the blade is sharp, the head is left smooth and ready for coloring. The head is colored with India ink and when dry, is rubbed with beeswax and burnished with a burnisher made for that purpose.

PLATE II

French Joint.

Now the book is marked for the French joint, that is, for the location of the back edges of the boards, and a strip of tough paper large enough to cover the back is glued on.

Glue is put into the open places left between the layers of the double boards; then the slips—super, tapes, and pieces of endpapers which were previously pasted together—are inserted into these openings, Fig. 23, and the book put into press, where it remains until thoroughly dry.

In putting on the boards, great care is necessary to insure a straight cover and perfect squares.

Half Leather.

It is now time to put on the leather, which is laid, flesh side up, on waste paper and thoroughly covered with paste. The waste paper is removed and the book is then placed in its proper position on the leather and the boards opened down against it with sufficient pressure to attach the leather to them. Then the ends of the leather are turned under the back of the book and over the boards, enclosing a cord at the head as shown at a, Fig. 24. This cord makes a roll instead of a headband. This done, the leather is thoroughly rubbed with the hands and forced closely down into the joints. Joint sticks, 10, Plate I, may be used for this purpose, but care must be used not to mar the leather with them. Now the book is placed with the foredge in the lying press, and a cord tied around it lengthwise through the joint to make sure than the leather holds its position at the joint. When dry, the leather is trimmed, since the work of getting it onto the book has probably stretched it, or the paring may have left the edges uneven.

Measurement is made from the foredge back to the points where it is desired to have the leather extend. With a sharp knife, the surplus leather is cut off. The book is now ready for the cover papers. Marks are made on the leather for the one-eighth inch lap of the paper.

Cover Paper.

The cover papers for the sides are cut one and one-half inches longer than the boards and seven-eighths of an inch wider than the distance from the leather to the foredge of the board. This allows three-fourths of an inch for turn-in and one-eighth of an inch for the lap over of the leather.

Then the book is placed on the paper, b, Fig. 24, in such manner as to have a straight edge of the paper come just to the marks on the leather and as nearly the same projection at the ends and foredge as possible. With a lead pencil, a line is drawn on the paper around the board. Corners for the mitres are cut, always cutting not closer to the pencil mark than the thickness of the board, as explained in the previous binding. This done, the paper is covered with paste, the book again laid on in position indicated by marks, and the turn-ins pasted.

The other board is now treated in the same manner. Great care is necessary to make sure that the paper fits firmly against the edge of the board. The bone folder is used here to force the paper against the edge of the board before the turn-in is pasted down on top.

The paper at the corners usually does not make a perfect mitre, but laps. This is remedied by taking a sharp knife and cutting through the lapping papers and removing the pieces cut off.

The book is now put under light pressure until dry. Nothing remains now but to paste the colored endpapers to the boards, the same as in the previous binding. It will be seen on opening the book how much flexibility the zigzag has lent to the cover.

IV.
EXTRA BINDING.

1.

Three-quarters Morocco.

2.

Sewed on cords; cords laced into boards.

3.

Flexible back.

4.

Edges cut in boards, head colored.

5.

Rounded and backed.

6.

Zigzag endpapers, colored pastedown.

7.

Head and foot bands, silk thread over heavy cords.

8.

Blind or gold tooled and lettered.

Cords.

The sewing frame is prepared exactly in the same way as in the Library Binding except that cords are here used instead of tapes, Fig. 25. Endpapers are cut and prepared zigzag, book marked up and punctures sawed the same as in the Library Binding.

These are the distinct differences between sewing on cords and on tapes. With cords, the needle goes in at the head puncture and out on the left of the cord and then doubles back and from the *right* of the cord, the needle is inserted at the same hole through which it came out, completely encircling the cord with the thread, a, Fig. 25. This is the whole story of sewing on cords. In the use of tapes, the thread simply goes back of the tapes, not around them. The kettlestitches are made just as in sewing on tapes, but there are no catch or crowfoot stitches as with tapes. When the book is taken from the sewing frame, the back is rounded. In this process, judgment must be used not to get the back too convex.

Fig. 25. Sewing on cords. a, stitch around the cord.

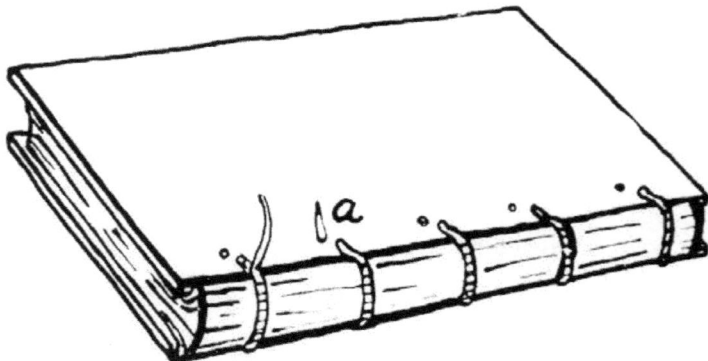

Fig. 26. Lacing cords into boards.

Fig. 27. Detail of holes and trough for cords.

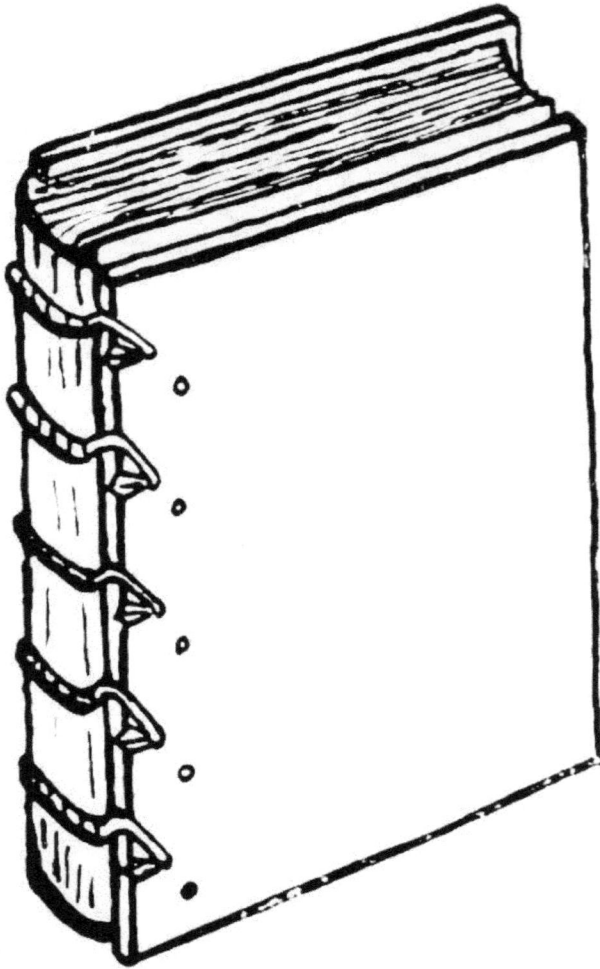

Fig. 28. Board pulled down ready for the head to be cut.

The book is now put into the backing boards in the press and glued and backed as described in dealing with the Library Binding.

Lacing Holes.

Two boards, as wide as the book and one-fourth of an inch longer, are cut from heavy tar or mill board. The boards are placed in proper position closely up against the joint projection of the back, and marks perpendicular to the back edges of the boards, are made, indicating the positions of the cords. At each mark and about one-half of an inch from the edge, a hole almost as large as the cords, is made with an awl from the outside, and the projections caused by the awl are trimmed off. Then about one-half inch from these holes, another row of somewhat smaller holes is made. These holes are not in the lines drawn from the edges of the boards, as is shown in Figs. 26 and 27, and are punched from the inside, leaving the projections caused by the awl.

Then a kind of V or trough is cut from each of the first series of holes to the edge of the board, making a place for the cord to lie, Fig. 27.

Lacing.

Now the cords are frayed out and trimmed thin at the ends, and with paste, the frayed portions are twisted to points and inserted down through the first holes and up through the others, a, Fig. 26. When the cords have been drawn tightly and a small amount of paste put around the holes, the ends are again frayed out and spread about the holes, and with a hammer, the board resting firmly on a block, the protruding parts of the board are pounded down about the cords. After this has been done to all the cords on both sides, the book is left to dry.

The cutting of the edges in boards, is a process requiring the greatest care. A mark is drawn on the white endpaper indicating where the head is to be cut. A tin and a piece of heavy cardboard are placed between the book and the back board. These make a cut-against to protect the cover from the knife. The front board is now drawn down even with the head mark, Fig. 28, and prepared in this way, the book is put into the cutting press.

It is essential to good work that the book be absolutely true in the press, and that the head mark and the top of the board which has been pulled down, be on a level with the top surface of the jaw of the press. The cutting is the same as described under Library Binding, page 27.

The book is now removed, the covers are thrown back, and with a try square against the head, a mark is drawn on the endpaper, showing where the foredge is to be cut. With the covers hanging down and a pressing board and one or two thicknesses of cardboard for a cut-against, the book is put into the press and the foredge cut. The foot is cut exactly as was the head.

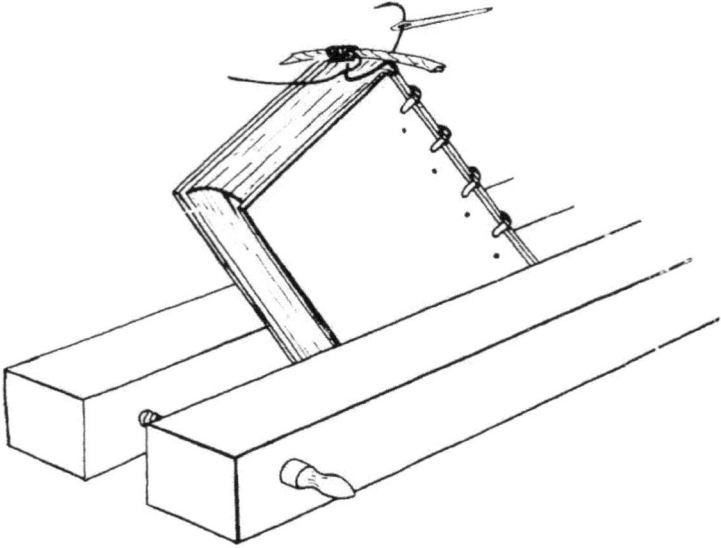

Fig. 29. Putting on the headband.

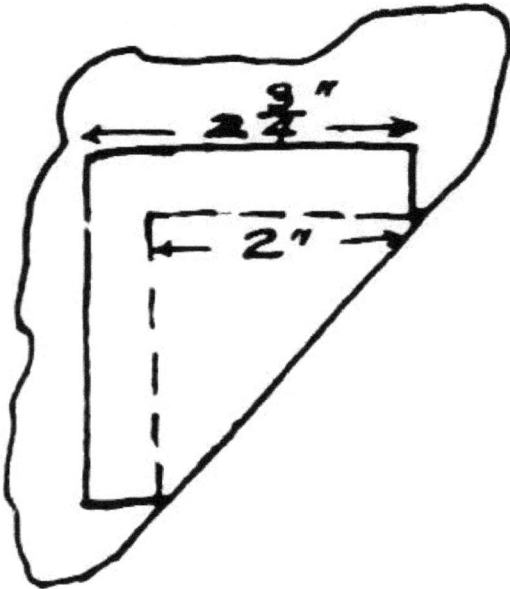

Fig. 30. Cutting the leather corners.

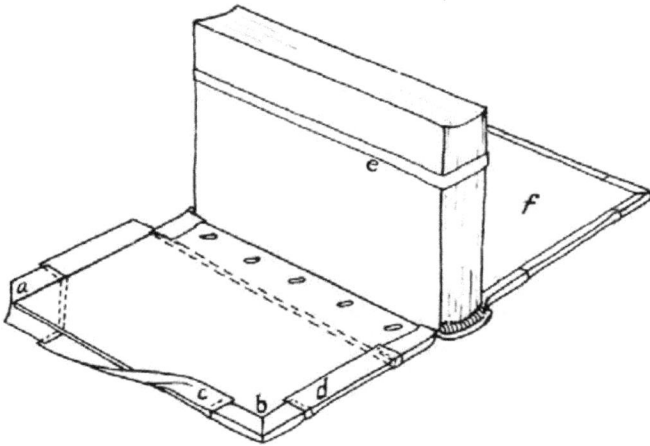

Fig. 31.
Pasting on leather corners and cover papers.
a, Turn-in of leather.
b, Turn-in mitre of leather.
c, and d, Turn-ins of paper.
e, Taper tied around book.
f, End pasted down.

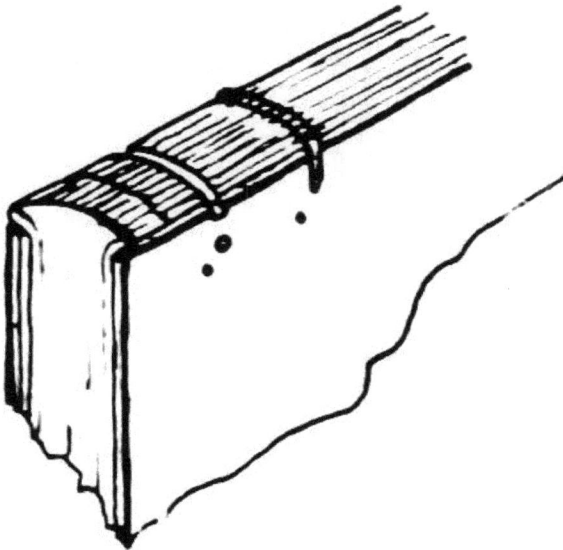

Fig. 32. Deep punctures for sunken cords.

Fig. 33. Folded paper for hollow back cover.

Head and Foot Bands.

It is now time to make the head and foot bands. The book is fastened in a lying press as shown in Fig. 29, with the head leaning toward the workman. A needle, into which is tied one end of a long, colored silk thread is run through the middle of the first section down to the head puncture and out through the back, the thread being drawn half its length through. Then a strong piece of cord, considerably longer than the width of the back, is laid on the head of the book just back of the boards. The needle end of the thread is brought directly forward over the cord, while the other end is crossed over the needle end of the thread, under the cord, and forward over the cord the same as the first thread. Then changing hands again, this operation is repeated twice when the needle is run down into the head of the book and out at the back one-half inch or more below the head but as it comes back over the cord, it is crossed by the other thread exactly as at first. About every fourth crossing, the thread should be sewed into the book.

When the cord is covered to the other side of the book, the two threads are knotted firmly beneath the cord. A small bit of paste is put at the end of the silk on each side, and the cord cut off. Then a tough piece of paper reaching from the top cord to the top of the headband is glued on to hold the band in place.

The foot band is made in exactly the same manner.

Then a strip of paper as wide as the back is glued on and carefully fitted about the cords.

Rubbing Sticks—Band Nippers.

The leather back is put on as in the Library Binding, but much greater care and patience are required in rubbing down the leather about the cords and making it adhere strongly to the book at all points. Rubbing sticks, 7, Plate I, come in good place in this operation. Band nippers are often used to force the leather against the cords. The leather is moistened slightly at the head and foot and made to lie down snugly against the head and foot bands. After this, the leather pieces for the corners are cut and marked up, leaving a three-quarter inch margin on the two equal sides of the triangle, Fig. 30. A general rule for the size of corners is that the altitude of the finished corner triangle should be about the same as the extension of the back leather over the side of the book.

Leather Corners.

The corners of the leather pieces are cut out just as the corners of the paper in the previous book. Then the edges are pared thin. The leather corners are covered with paste, one at a time, a corner of the cover board is placed in proper position on the leather and the turn-ins pasted, a and b, Fig. 31. This done, the book is put under light pressure for a time. The leather is now all trimmed to proper size and the cover paper marked and cut for the sides. The one-eighth inch lap is marked on the leather back, and the book laid on the paper as in previous book. Then with a sharp pencil, points are made on the paper showing where it must be cut to allow not more than one-eighth inch lap on the leather of the corners, Fig. 31.

The corners of the paper are cut out, the paper covered with paste, the book placed in proper position and the turn-ins pasted as at c and d. Care must again be exercised that the paper comes squarely against the edges of the boards and fits closely around the edges of the leather. For such processes, the bone folder is almost indispensable.

The next step is the lining of the boards. A rectangular piece of heavy paper is pasted on the inside of each cover and fitted snugly against the edges of the leather and paper turn-ins. After these linings are dry, the end papers are trimmed and pasted down. In this case, great care and patience are necessary to make the endpapers attach themselves to the back edges of the boards. Of course, the outside white leaves are torn off and the colored pastedowns are drawn back upon the boards as in the Library Binding, and with a bone folder, the papers are forced against the back edges of the boards. Then the book is closed and immediately opened. If in closing, the endpaper is pulled loose or wrinkled, it is again put into proper order and the book again closed.

When the end papers hold their positions perfectly, the book is thoroughly protected with paper, tins and boards and put lightly into press.

Then the head is colored with India ink, a coat of beeswax put on, and a burnisher used to give it a polish. It is well to leave the completed book under some pressure for several days.

If, in the process, some paste has gotten on the leather or paper, it may be removed by the use of a damp cloth, carefully rubbed over the soiled places.

Hollow Back.

In case a hollow back is desired for this book, deep punctures are sawed at every cord, and the cords which are smaller than in the flexible binding, are sunken into these punctures, Fig. 32. The sewing in such a binding is very simple, the thread running along the middle of the section and behind the cords, with kettlestitches at the head and foot, the same as in the flexible sewing.

Before the cover goes on, a heavy paper folded as in Fig. 33, making from three to five thicknesses, is glued by the bottom layer to the back.

But especially in elementary work where very little gold tooling and lettering are undertaken, the hollow back is neither necessary nor desirable. At all events, let us avoid the false cords sometimes seen in commercial books.

V.
REBINDING.

The foregoing work has assumed that the books were to be bound from the original, unfolded sheets.

In case of rebinding books, the following preliminary steps are necessary before beginning the sewing:—

1. Taking off old cover. This is done simply by pulling loose the endpapers and carefully loosening the super. If the glue or paste refuses to come off, it is covered with a coat of fresh paste, and after a short time may be scraped off.

2. Cutting sections apart. The leaves are counted until the thread is reached which indicates the middle of the section. The thread is clipped and the same number of leaves, disregarding plates, is counted, bringing us to the end of the section. The counting is necessary because of the fact that in many books, the first and last few sections are pasted, or tipped, together, making it difficult to tell where one stops and the other begins.

3. Beating out the joint. In books which have been rounded and backed, the first and last few sections especially have a decided bend near the backs caused by the hammering. This is removed by laying the sections down on a solid block and hammering them along the joints.

4. Mending, cleaning and guarding. Guards are strips of tough paper about one-fourth of an inch wide which are used to paste together the leaves of a folio that have been torn apart, and to fasten plates into the book. In case of the torn folio, the leaves are laid side by side in the proper position and a guard, covered with paste, is placed over the joint where the leaves come together. The leaves are then folded together creasing the guard in the middle. This general rule as to the placing of the guards is given in the form of a bull:—"If it is to be guarded on the outside, put the guard on the inside; but if it is to be guarded on the inside, put the guard on the outside." That is, if it is the outside folio of the section to be guarded, put the guard on the inside of the folio, so that the ragged edges of the tear may be gathered up by the glue on the back and that it may not interfere with the sewing. But if it is an inside folio to be guarded, put the guard or the outside of the folio. When guarding in a plate, a folio is opened out, the plate placed on the proper leaf, and the guard put on as in the case of a torn folio.

5. Cutting new end papers.

After all the foregoing steps, the book is ready to be pressed, placing the sections upon each other and inserting tins and boards as described in Case Binding.

When it comes to re-sewing the book and putting on new covers, the practice is to use any method or any combination of methods that seems to be demanded by the conditions and size of the book, and the character of usage which it will probably meet. It is not unusual in commercial binderies to sew books especially large, heavy books, on tapes or on sunken cords without regard to the style of cover. This is done especially where the book has large, thick sections that are difficult to hold in place. Thus it is seen how far, under some conditions, we depart from the standard types.

It sometimes happens that the folios are so badly torn at the folds that to guard them would make the back unusually thick. In such cases, the overcasting method is used. The back of the book is cut if it is in very bad condition, and then instead of sewing through punctures over cords or tapes, several of the leaves are taken and placed in the same position as a section, and sewed through, whipping over and over, and going around tapes or cords in the usual manner. It frequently happens however, that a book is in good condition with the exception of the cover, in which case, simply a new cover is put on. This necessitates re-gluing of the back and putting on new super and end papers. Then the question arises how to fasten in the end papers so that they may be strong. One method, especially in the case of heavy books, is to put in a cloth joint. This is a folded strip of cloth about one inch wide, at each end of the book, with one side of the fold pasted to the outside leaf. Then when the cover is put on, the other side of the cloth fold is pasted to the board, Fig. 34. A folio of cover paper is then tipped against the cloth and the outside leaf pasted to the board; or in many cases, a separate sheet is used for the pastedown, leaving both leaves of the end folio free.

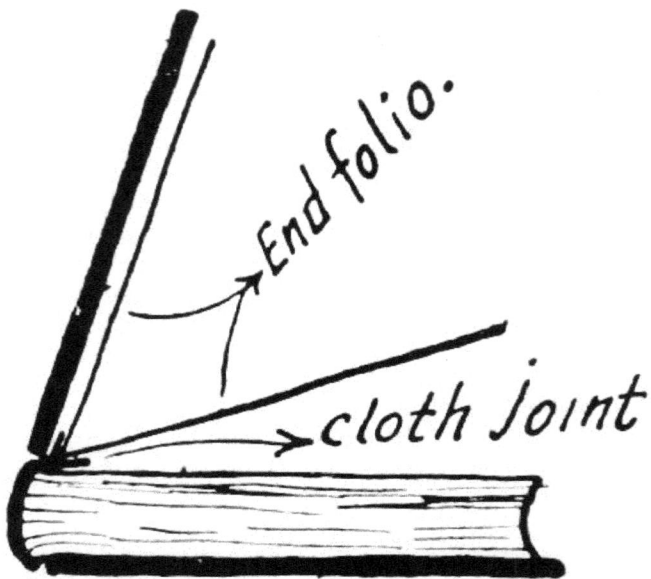

Fig. 34.

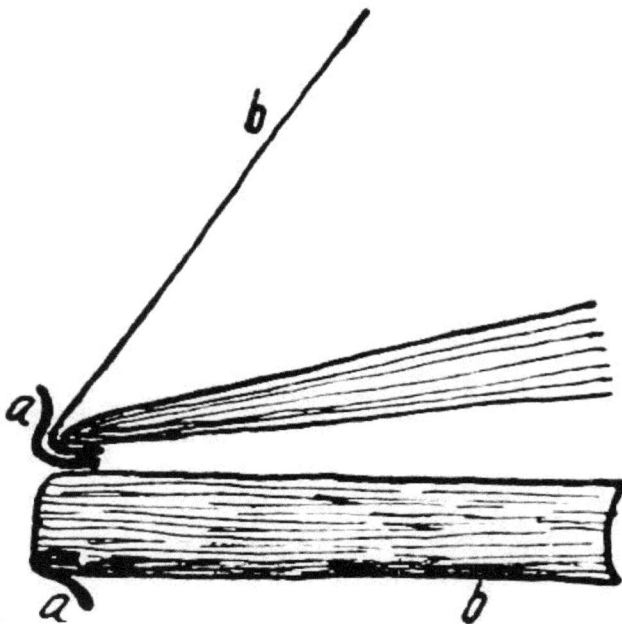

Fig. 35.
a, Cloth joints b, End sheets

In the case of marbled endpapers, the folio is cut of paper to match the book, a piece of super or canvass is put along the fold like a guard, then the single sheet of marbled paper is pasted entirely over the first page of the folio which is then tipped in to the cloth of the joint. Where a book is to be resewed, sometimes single end sheets of heavy cover stock, together with the cloth for the joint, are folded around the backs of the first and last sections and sewed in with them, Fig. 35. Then when the boards are put on, the cloth is drawn back over the edge as before.

Another method of attempting to reinforce and strengthen the first and last parts of a book is to sew through the endpapers that are to remain free as "flyleaves" and the leaves of the first half of the first and last sections. This seems of somewhat doubtful value, although it may be of some service in the case of a thick, heavy book.

A very practical and easy method of rebinding moderately thin books which have torn backs, is to sew them in the manner described for a fourth-grade Language Book, Fig. 40, page 55, and put on a new case binding. In such cases, care must be used to make the joint wide enough to allow the boards to come well in front of the stitches; otherwise, the book would not open without tearing the cover.

Plate III shows a number of library books rebound in this manner by seventh grade boys.

PLATE III

Library Books Rebound by Seventh Grade Boys.

VI.
EQUIPMENT.

Equipment for elementary bookbinding, as already indicated in a preceding chapter, can be made almost entirely to fit the purse.

The statement occurs in text books and has gone the rounds on "good authority" that very little can be done in the way of bookbinding without a large and unusually expensive equipment. It is difficult to understand how such a statement could be made by anyone who is familiar with craft binding and its simplified forms as they may be worked out in the lower grades of our schools.

Of course, it is possible to spend any amount for bookbinding equipment, but there are many schools where good elementary work is being done with absolutely no equipment except pocket knives, scissors and such other aids as may be picked up about any school building.

It is entirely possible to adjust the upper grade work so that only a few will be handling the same processes at the same time, thus making a small equipment answer the purposes of a good sized class.

For making the typical books under good conditions with a moderate number of pupils in the eighth grade or high school, the following equipment may be said to be elaborate, and can be had for about $75:—

1	10-inch Card Cutter,
6	Lying Presses,
1	Plow and Press,
2	Letter Presses,

12	Sewing Frames,
2	Paring Knives,
3	Pairs Backing Boards,
2	Back Saws,
6	Try Squares,
3	Hammers,
3	Doz. Pressing Boards and Tins,
6	Awls,
6	Paste Brushes,
12	Bone Folders.

Even this equipment may be very materially reduced. Many of the items may be improvised, made, or furnished by the pupils.

For instance, the sewing frames are of simple construction and offer an excellent problem for the class in woodwork.

The plow and press are not an essential even in high school work. Most excellent work may be done by cutting both paper and boards with a sharp knife guided by a trysquare or straight edge, against a cutting tin. Any ordinary hammer will do for backing purposes. So this brings us back to the repeated proposition that much and good bookbinding can be done in the schools with almost no equipment.

VII.
SUGGESTIVE COURSE.

In the previous discussions of the three main types of books, practically every process used in elementary hand-binding has been described.

The following outline is the result of several years of effort on the part of the author, to develop a series of problems involving the bookbinding processes, meeting some of the constructive needs of the various grades of the school, and relating in some vital way to the regular school interests.

It was thought that confusion would be avoided by indicating the methods and processes of a set of specific problems. It is understood that these problems are only typical and that from these, a great variety of books may be worked out in response to special needs. In the practical work of the class, these problems are not dictated step by step and in detail, to the pupils; but as far as possible each pupil plans for himself, size, number of pages, proportions, color combinations, decoration, etc. A very large part of the value derived from such work, comes from the necessity of thinking and planning in advance, and from the privilege and exercise of choice.

Let us assume that we are taking the problem of the fourth grade spelling book, page 53, Fig. 38. The first thing necessary is the spelling paper as a basis for our plans.

Each child is given a sheet of paper, say $3\frac{1}{2}\times8$ inches. The class is questioned to bring out the general characteristics of the cover needed, such as the direction of opening, the necessity for a hinge in the top cover, etc.

Then the matter of the squares or the extension of the boards is taken up and the pupils express opinions as to the amount of the extension. After reasons are given for various opinions, the pupils calculate and write on the sheets of paper the sizes the boards are to be cut.

Then comes the question of the distance the hinge is to be from the back. One pupil may answer three inches and another one-half an inch. Reasons are brought out why neither is satisfactory and also why it may vary, say, from three-fourths of an inch to one and one-half inches, and each child writes on his paper the distance he prefers. The same plan is used with reference to the width of the hinge; and since this may vary greatly, even from one-fourth to two inches, guided always by the ideas of good proportion and fulfillment of purposes, the pupils are asked to write down their preferences.

Then is taken up the question of the proportion of cloth to paper on the covers. In the first place, it is apparent that constructive considerations demand that the cloth must reach from the back some distance beyond the hinge toward the foredge, but how far beyond is a question of good proportion. It is always found that children vary but little in their judgments of proportion in this matter. The author has made this proposition to scores of children:—"Let's have the cloth and the cover paper meet at the middle of the cover," and in the whole number of children, there has never been one who would agree to any such an arrangement. When the matter of the cloth has been determined, the pupils calculate the sizes the pieces of cloth and paper must be cut, allowing the proper turn-ins. These dimensions are written down with the other decided points. From this information, the pupils make simple drawings. From samples of various colors of cloth, paper, and cords, the pupils select satisfactory combinations. In this, as in all other matters, if pupils make wrong selections or show poor judgment, it is the opportunity of the teacher to suggest and to convince them of the wisdom of some other choice.

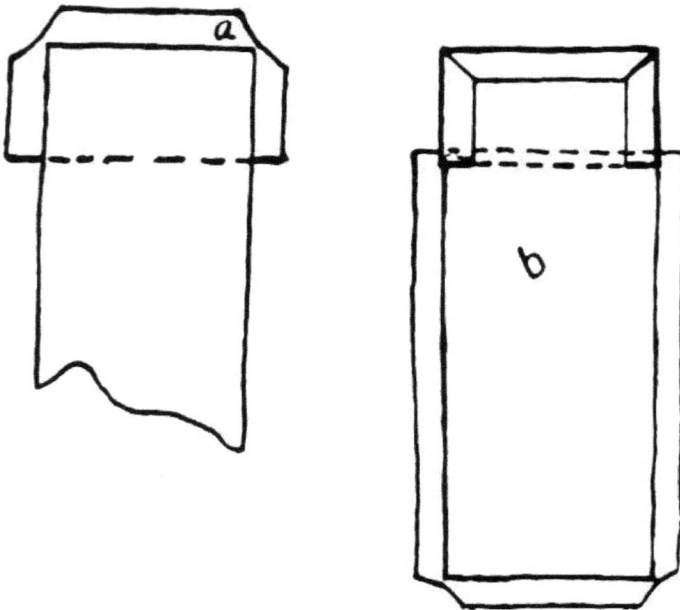

Fig. 36.

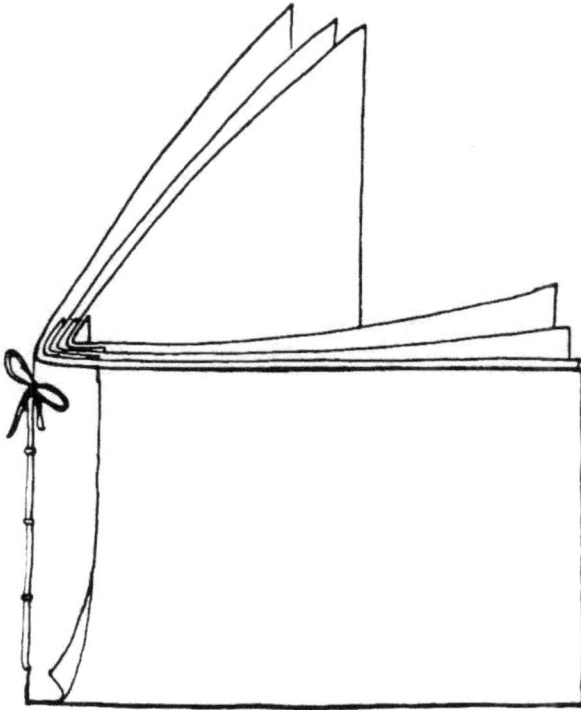

Fig. 37.

The material is next marked out and cut. Of course, this is done by each pupil from the information he has written on his sheet of paper.

The actual pasting of the boards into the cloth and paper requires but few suggestions or directions if the pupils have gone through the work of the previous grades. If they have not, then they are asked to place the board upon the cloth in the proper position, mark around it, and clip out corners as at a, Fig. 36. When the cloth is pasted on, the same process is used with the paper allowing it to lap one-eighth to one-fourth of an inch on the cloth, b. When the covers are completed and pressed, the punctures are made and the cord tied in.

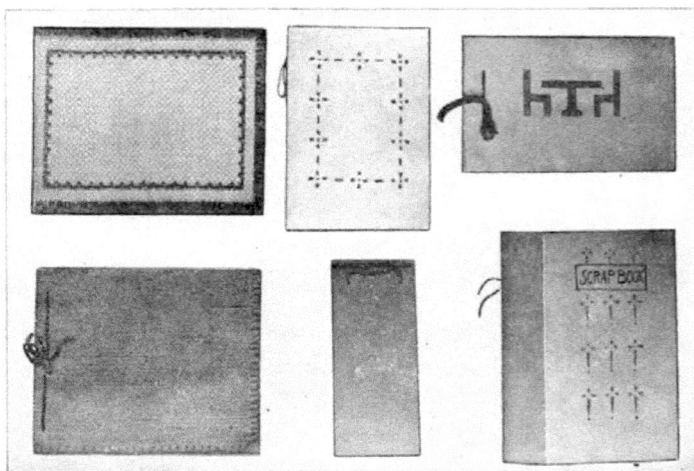

PLATE IV

1. Tilo Matting Poem Book   2. Nature or Sketch Book   3. Home Book

FIRST GRADE.

1. Home Book.

This is made to contain the freehand cuttings of the house and its furnishings, the family, the barn, the chicken house, all the animals, machinery, etc., about the home. It is made up of sheets of manila paper with colored sheets of the same size for covers. These are all tied together with a heavy cord through two holes punched at one end. 3, Plate IV.

2. Nature or Sketch Book.

Made of the same material as the Home Book except that only one colored sheet is needed. But the sheets are all folded in the middle and three or four punctures are made with a darning needle or a punch along the fold. A cord threaded into a large needle is run into the top puncture and out at the bottom puncture; then back into the second puncture from the bottom around the thread and out at the same puncture. This is repeated at each puncture until the top one is reached, where the ends of the cord are tied together, 2, Plate IV. The book may be made by finding the middle of the paper, punching the holes and tying the cord before the folding is done.

3. Portfolio.

This is made of two sheets of paper, one of which is one-half inch narrower and one inch shorter than the other. The small one is placed upon the large one in such a way as to leave a half inch strip around three sides. The two corners of the large sheet are cut out and the edges pasted and folded over upon the small sheet.

SECOND GRADE.

1. Portfolio.

Made of one piece of tough paper by simply cutting rectangles from the lower corners of the sheet, as shown in Fig. 37 A, and folding the rectangles a, b, c on dotted lines. The two smaller rectangles are pasted to the larger one, c.

2. Scrap Book.

Made of single leaves with a two-inch fold at one end. Covered with a folio of Bristol, reinforced at the back with strip of book cloth, and tied through five punctures with heavy cord. Fig. 37. See 6, Plate IV.

3. Nature Book.

Cover same as Scrap Book with the addition of pieces of cover paper pasted on the covers, reaching from the cloth to the foredge. Book made of folios sewed like 2, grade one. Pasted into cover.

4. Spelling Book Cover.

Made of light boards which are covered with cover paper. Pieces of cover paper are pasted on the inside as end papers, and are decorated by the children. The two sides of the cover are fastened together by inserting rings or cords in holes punched at the end. 5, Plate IV.

5. Language, Poem or Arithmetic Book.

Single leaves covered with folio of crash or burlap, tied with cord through three punctures, cover lined with one piece of cover paper, and edges and design of cover worked with coarse thread. 4, Plate IV.

THIRD GRADE.

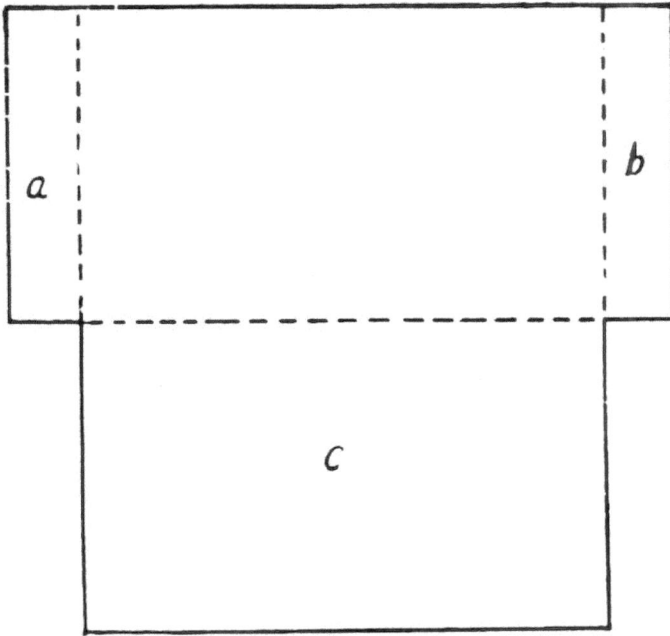

Fig. 37A.

1. Spelling Book.

Single leaves with separate boards, covered with book cloth pasted all over. The top board is cut into two parts, leaving a flexible hinge near the back. Boards lined with cover paper. Tied through two, three or four punctures by Japanese method, Fig. 38.

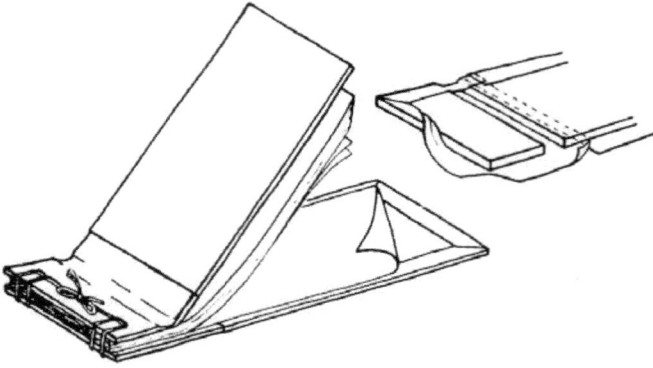

Fig. 38.

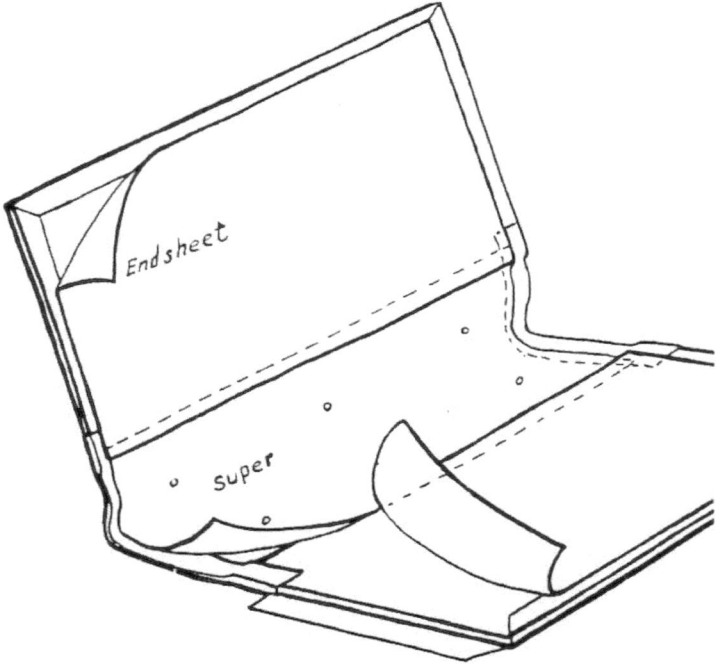

Fig. 39.

2. Literature Illustration Book Cover.

Half cloth. Narrow boards, leaving wide limp back of book cloth. Back reinforced with super and boards lined with cover paper. Two or three boles are punched from side to side, and tied with heavy cord or fastened with rings. Fig. 39.

3. Portfolio.

Made of one long, narrow piece of cover paper or Manila board. The bottom third is folded up to form the body of the portfolio, and the top third is folded down for the hap or cover. Two strips of cloth are folded and pasted to the ends of the portfolio to hold the front and back together.

4. Nature Book.

One section sewed with five punctures, same as number 2, grade one, covered with heavy marbled boards, with buckram back, super put on, and first and last leaves used as pastedowns.

5. Poem Book Cover.

Made of two boards. Joint made in top board as in Spelling Book. Boards are covered with crash and lined inside with cover paper. Tied with heavy cord through four punctures.

6. Japanese Book.

The book part is made by folding a long piece of paper first one way and then the other until it is all folded accordion fashion. Boards are covered with cover paper and pasted to the first and last pages.

FOURTH GRADE.

1. Portfolio.

Made of heavy cover paper, with some method devised by the class for increasing and decreasing the thickness of the portfolio.

2. Clipping Envelope.

Made of one piece of heavy cover paper or light Manila board. Rectangles a little longer than half the body of the envelope, are folded over and pasted. The small flap at the bottom is folded up and pasted. See Fig. 39 A.

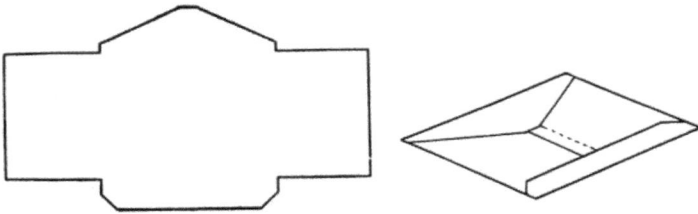

Fig. 39A.

3. Spelling Book.

Same as that of third grade except with half instead of full cloth covers. See Fig. 38.

4. Language, Geography or History Notebook.

More than one section. Sheets folded and cut. Sections arranged in book form, and a colored folio tipped in to the second endpaper on each side. The book is marked up for a sawed puncture one-half inch from each end, and for stabs immediately under the sawed punctures and every half inch along the side and about one-fourth of an inch from the back, a, Fig. 40. The stabs are made with a sharp punch or awl.

A needle is put on each end of a long linen thread. Then with the thread lying in the head puncture, a needle is inserted from each side into the head stab and the thread drawn through. The needles are then run into the next stab and then into the next, until the foot puncture is reached. Here the threads are brought up and tied so that the knot sinks into the sawed puncture.

Fig. 40.

A piece of super is now thoroughly pasted upon the back and about one and one-half inches down the endpapers. These outside leaves of the endpapers are cut off at the front edge of the super and a piece of the cover paper as long as the book and as wide as the super is glued on, b, care being taken to have it fit flat across the back with sharp turns at the edges.

The boards having been covered separately, except lining, are now pasted on about three-eighths of an inch from the back or one-eighth of an inch in front of the stitches. The book is now put lightly into press. When dry, the colored endpapers are pasted to the covers and the book again put into press.

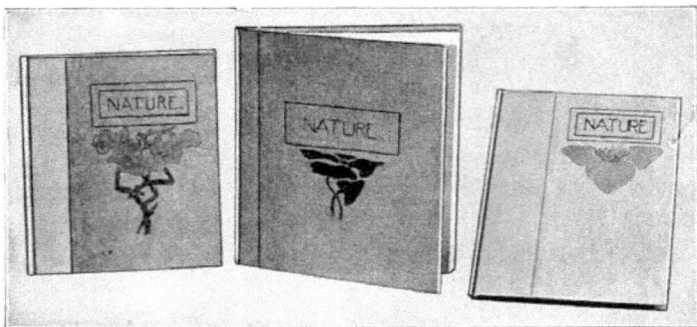

Fig. 41.

FIFTH GRADE.

1. Nature Book.

One section. Large sheet folded and cut or torn to proper size. Sewed through five punctures. Bound in full or half cloth. Case binding. Super put on and first and last leaves pasted to covers by closing the cover on the paste-covered endpapers. Fig. 41.

2. Spelling Pad.

Made like the top cover of the spelling book shown at Fig. 38, except that it has cloth corners, which are put on the same as the leather corners of the Extra Binding, Fig. 31. Four punctures are made and the narrow part is turned over and tied as at Fig. 42.

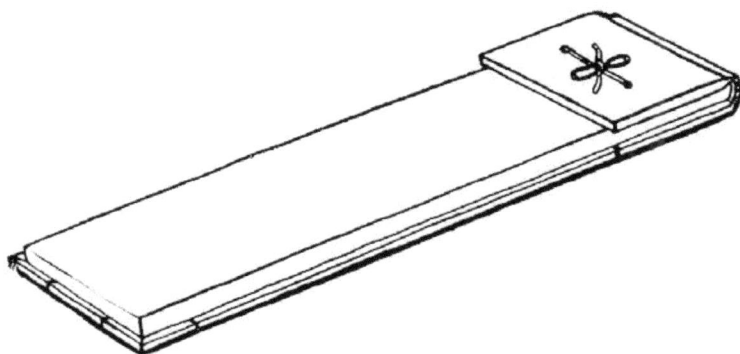

Fig. 42.

Spelling Pad

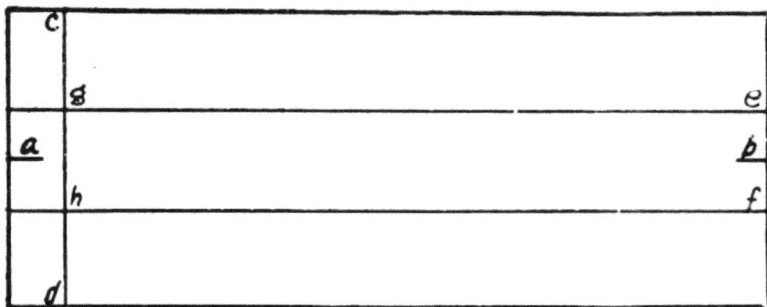

Fig. 42A.

3. Soft Leather Cover.

This makes a nice gift for Christmas. The cover is removed from a small book, a folio of cover paper is tipped to each side for end papers, and the book is pasted into a cover of velvet sheep skin.

4. Re-cover.

Some library book or book of the pupil's.

New super put on, new endpapers tipped in, and a new half cloth case binding made and laid on. Boards as wide as the book and three-eighths of an inch longer. Cloth as wide as desired and one and one-half inches longer than the boards. Cover paper as long as the cloth and seven-eighths of an inch wider than the distance from the back cloth to the foredge of the board. Cloth is folded lengthwise and creased only at the ends, as at a and b, Fig. 42 A. A line c d is drawn ¾ from one end. Lines h f and g e are drawn. The distance of these lines from a and b is half the thickness of the book, plus one joint. The boards are pasted into the angles d h f and c g e, and the cover is put lightly into press. The cover paper is marked up and pasted on exactly as described in Library Binding, page <u>30</u>.

5. Post Card Book.

Loose leaves of cover paper 7"×11". Cover made exactly like the fourth grade spelling book at Fig. 38, except that it must be much larger in order to accommodate the larger leaves.

Various devices may be used to hold the cards, but the best method perhaps, is to cut slits for the corners.

6. Rebind Straight Back Book.

a.

Old cover torn off.

b.

Sections cut apart.

c.

Mended and guarded.

d.

Endpapers cut.

e.

Sewed all along with five punctures. Consult Case Binding, Fig. 14.

f.

Back glued.

g.

Half cloth case binding made and put on.

7. Magazine Cover.

Case binding in full cloth. Inside of back lined with a strip of book cloth. A one inch piece of cloth or leather runs lengthwise inside of each board to hold the leaves of the magazine. These strips are fastened by turning the ends and pasting them under the end papers, similar to that shown in photograph, Fig. 52.

8. Art Book.

Several sections sewed all along. Heavy gray paper for mounting drawings and pictures. Original work on cover, using combinations and modifications of previous problems. After the book is bound, a sufficient number of leaves may be cut out along through the book to prevent too great thickness at the back.

SIXTH GRADE.

1. Portfolio.

Simply a case binding in half or full cloth, with a cloth pocket inside of each cover. Each pocket is made by taking a piece of cloth one inch wider and two inches longer than the board, and folding the edges of one side and the two ends and pasting to the board. Then the cover is finished according to the method of making a case binding.

2. Memorandum Book.

One section with a small folio of Manila board outside. Cover is made of one piece of buffing, which is cut ¾" longer and wider than the finished cover. A piece of tough paper exactly the size of the finished cover, is pasted on the inside of the buffing, leaving about a three-eighths inch margin all round. A piece of Manila board as wide as the paper, is laid on the paper at each end. These boards should be short enough to leave a three-quarter inch space at the middle of the leather for the back.

The projecting edges of the leather are now turned over and pasted to the Manila board. End papers as long as the Manila boards and one-fourth inch narrower, are now pasted on. After the cover has dried in press, the ends of the outside folio of the book are inserted under the unpasted ends of the Manila boards of the cover.

3. Binding from Original Printed Sheets.

Small book like "Printing and Bookbinding," "He Knew Lincoln," "Man Without a Country," or "The Other Wise Man." Arrangements can be made with publishers to furnish unfolded printed sheets at reasonable prices.

Sheets are folded and pressed—not cut.

Sewed all along with five punctures.

Typical case binding.

Full cloth.

Edges untrimmed.

4. Rebind Sets of Books.

Case bindings in full cloth, each pupil making a number of covers at one time.

Where several books are to be uniformly bound, a spacer is used to locate the positions of the boards on the cloth, instead of repeating the measurements on each cover. The spacer, Fig. 43, may be made of press board, tin, celluloid, or other material. By placing the spacer at the middle of the cloth at the head, the angles are located for the corners of the boards.

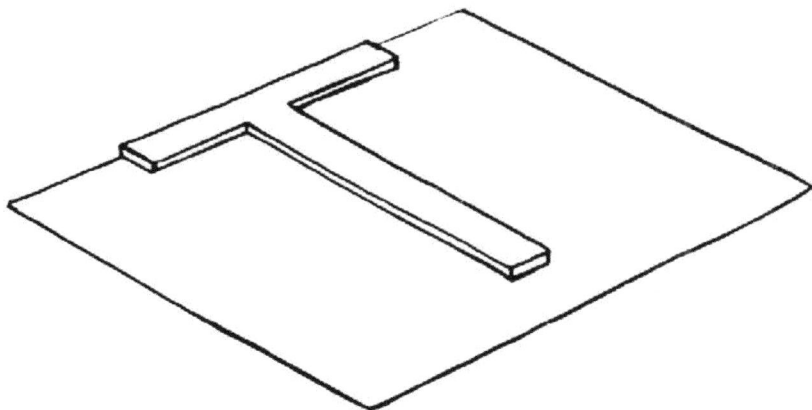

Fig. 43.

5. Envelope File.

A number of envelopes are made according to the plan indicated by Fig. 39 A, page 55. With two pieces of cloth folded back and forth, the ends of the envelopes are bound together as shown in Fig. 44.

A case binding in half cloth is made similar to the Literature Illustration Book, Fig. 39, making plenty of allowance at the back for the thickness of the envelopes. When the cover is completed, the bottom envelope is pasted firmly to one of the boards, as shown at Fig. 45.

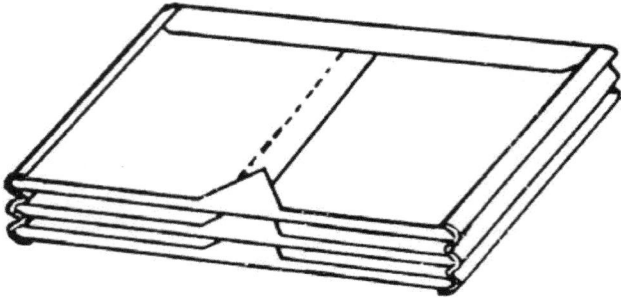

Fig. 44.

Envelope File

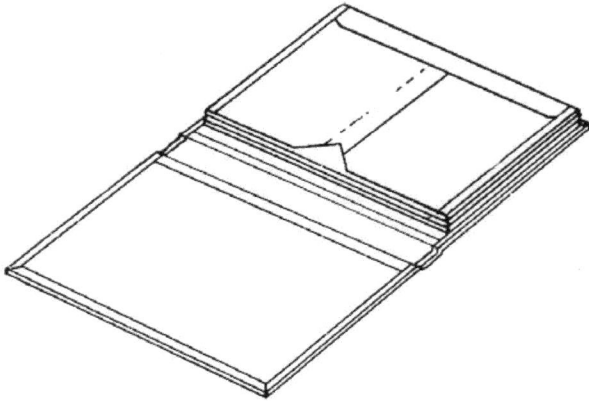

Fig. 45.

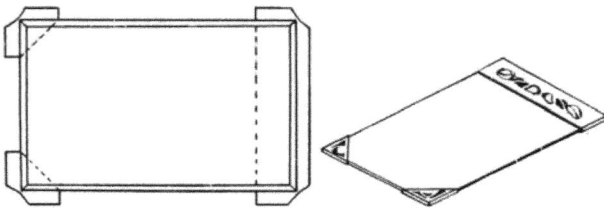

Desk Pad

Fig. 46.

6. Desk Pad.

Made of one piece of heavy cloth board. A piece of cover paper one and one-half inches longer and wider than the board, is pasted to one side and the edges turned over. Thin leather corners or end strips are now put on as indicated at Fig. 46, with only the turnovers pasted. Then the under side of the board is covered with a piece of cover paper about one-half inch shorter and narrower than the board.

The leather may be decorated by tooling, cutting, or coloring.

7. Note Book Cover.

Stiff boards with cloth back and corners, and paper sides. Corners are put on the same as the leather corners in the Extra Binding, Fig. 31.

Two strips of board are cut three-quarters of an inch wide, and one inch shorter than the cover. A piece of cloth is cut as long as the strips of board and four inches wider than the back of the cover. One of these strips of board is now pasted one-half inch from each long edge of the cloth. The other sides of the strips of board are covered with paste and the cloth is folded over upon them.

Fig. 47 shows the end of this part which is pasted inside of the back of the cover, the one-half inch projections of the cloth being attached firmly to the boards. End papers are put in and holes for the cord are now punched through these three-quarter inch strips, and the leaves are tied in place. Finished cover shown at Fig. 48.

Fig. 47.

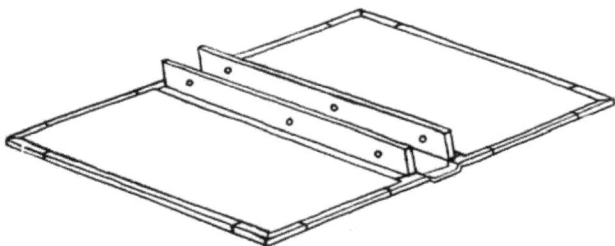

Fig. 48.

SEVENTH GRADE.

1. Decorative Binding.

Blank book or magazines sewed on colored tapes, ribbons or strips of leather with coarse silk thread in decorative stitches, Fig. 49.

Boards are bound separately in fancy cover papers.

Tapes are laced through the boards and tied at foredge. Colored endpapers pasted to covers.

Tapes and stitches left exposed at back.

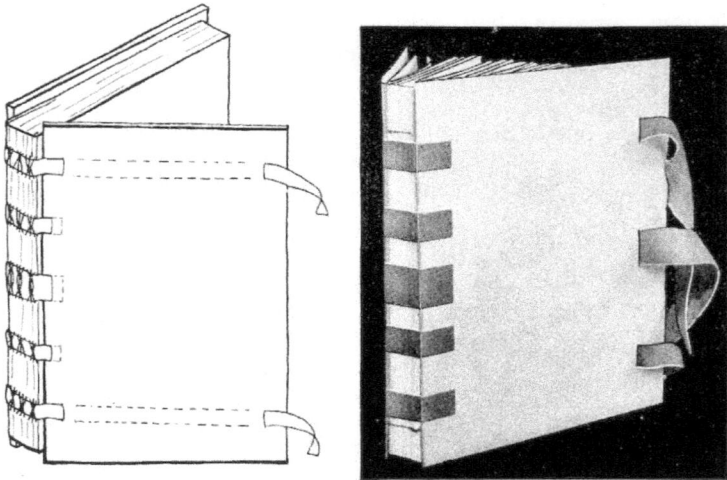

Fig. 49.

2. Portfolio.

Three rectangular pieces of tar or cloth board are cut, two larger ones for the body of the portfolio and one smaller one for the lid or flap. The large pieces are lined with paper on the sides which are to go inside. This prevents warping when the outside covering is put on. A strip of book cloth or buckram is cut about two inches wide and long enough to reach around one side and the two ends of the body of the portfolio. This strip is folded lengthwise in the middle with the wrong side out. Then each half is folded lengthwise in the middle, turning the wrong side in.

Thus folded, the strip is pasted around the ends and bottom edges of the two large boards, mitering all the corners. Fig. 50. Then the flap is attached by means of two strips of cloth, one above and one below, and the edges are bound to correspond with the body. Then cover paper is pasted on all the uncovered surfaces of the boards, lapping one-eighth of an inch over the edges of the cloth wherever the paper and cloth come together. Scores of modifications may be made of this style of portfolio.

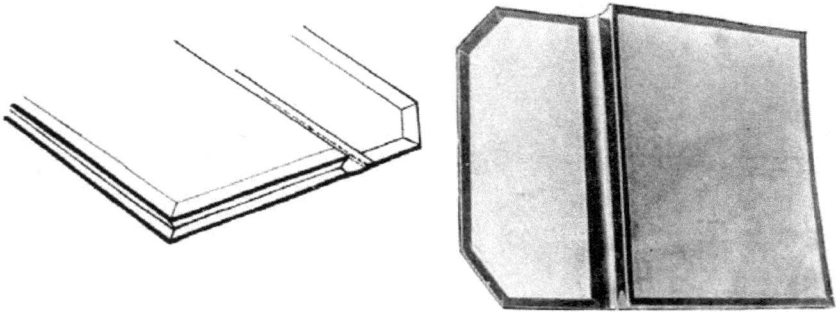

Fig. 50.

Showing only the cloth on the edges.

3. Limp Leather Binding.

Pupil's blank or printed book.

Sewed all along or on tapes. Colored endpapers sewed in. Bound in one piece of sheep or calf. Cover is used for dyeing and tooling in decoration. Book put into cover by pasting book and fitting leather closely about it and then pressing.

EIGHTH GRADE.

1. Book for Mounting Drawings and Pictures.

Heavy cover paper is used for this book and is cut into large folios. Then strips of the same paper about one and one-half inches wide and as long as the book is high, are folded lengthwise in the middle. One of these folded strips is fitted over the back and one inside of each folio, Fig. 51, except the first and last. This provides for the pasting of a mount on each page of the book without making the body of the book thicker than the back. Sewed on tapes. Cover treated exactly as that of the Library Binding, page 27.

Fig. 51

It is much easier to handle this problem by making the book of regular sections instead of using the one and one-half inch strips, and then cutting out every 3rd or 4th leaf after it is completed. These leaves are not wasted. They may be used for smaller books.

2. Typical Library Binding. See page 22.

Half leather.

Sewed on tapes.

Double boards.

French joint.

Backed and rounded.

Head cut and colored.

Cord inserted instead of headband.

3. Portfolio.

Bound in leather and paper or cloth. Three boards are cut the same size. The joints between the boards are treated exactly like the back of a case binding, except that leather is used and that the inside of the joints are also lined up with leather. Small boards for the flaps are joined in the same manner to the ends of the middle board. Fig. 52 shows the portfolio with only the leather pasted on. The cover paper or cloth is cut and pasted exactly like that of the Library or Extra Binding.

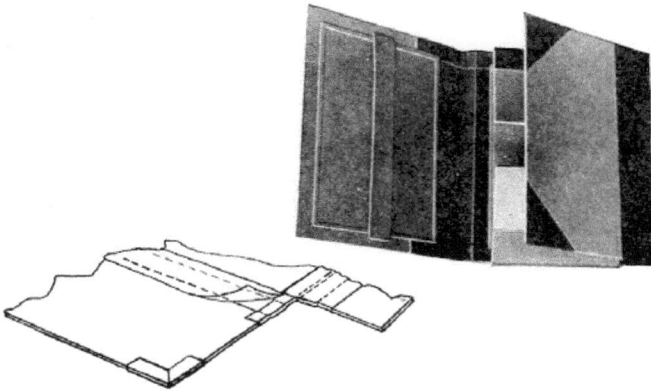

Fig. 52. Showing part of portfolio with only the leather pasted on.

Milton Keynes UK
Ingram Content Group UK Ltd.
UKHW030625061024
449204UK00004B/313

9 789362 514592